I0479348

A
Journey
of Colors! Vol. I

Adult Coloring Book

A coloring journey of adventure and relaxation, using new techniques, and original images to teach beginners, and entertain experts.

To get more information and updates, and be at the front row of our adventure to InspireLife, visit us at:
www.InspireLife.nft

You will have to use Brave Browser or Opera Browser to access the website above. Thank you.

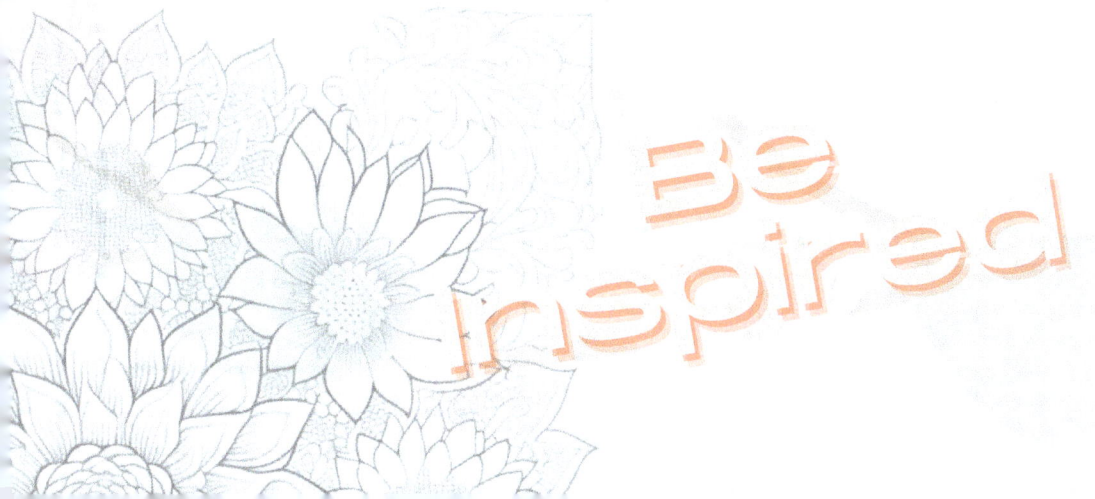

Be Inspired

Hey,

Are you human?

Then we love you!

This Book Belongs to:

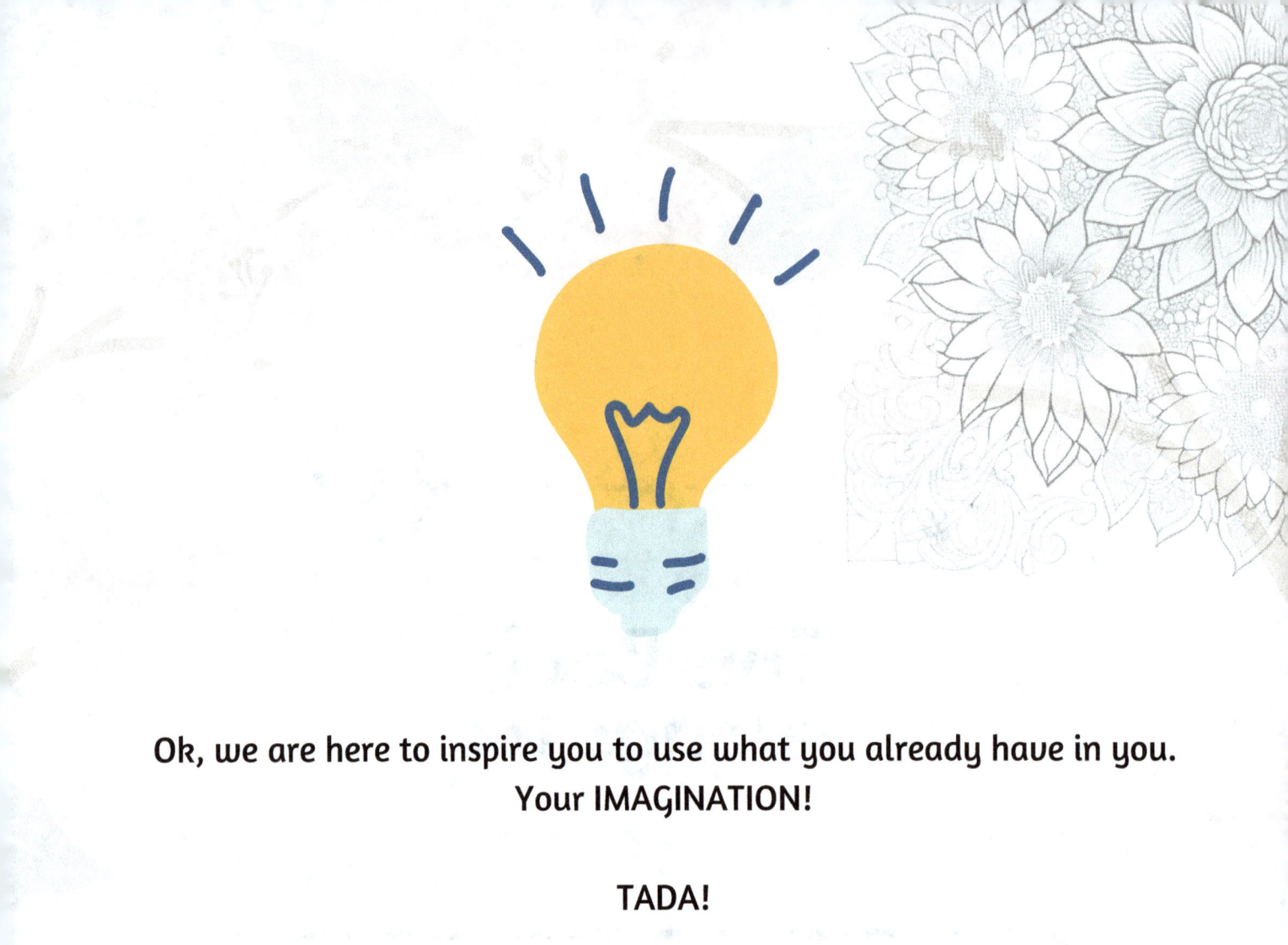

Ok, we are here to inspire you to use what you already have in you.
Your IMAGINATION!

TADA!

Take a careful look at this image, and notice the color arrangement and segmentation.

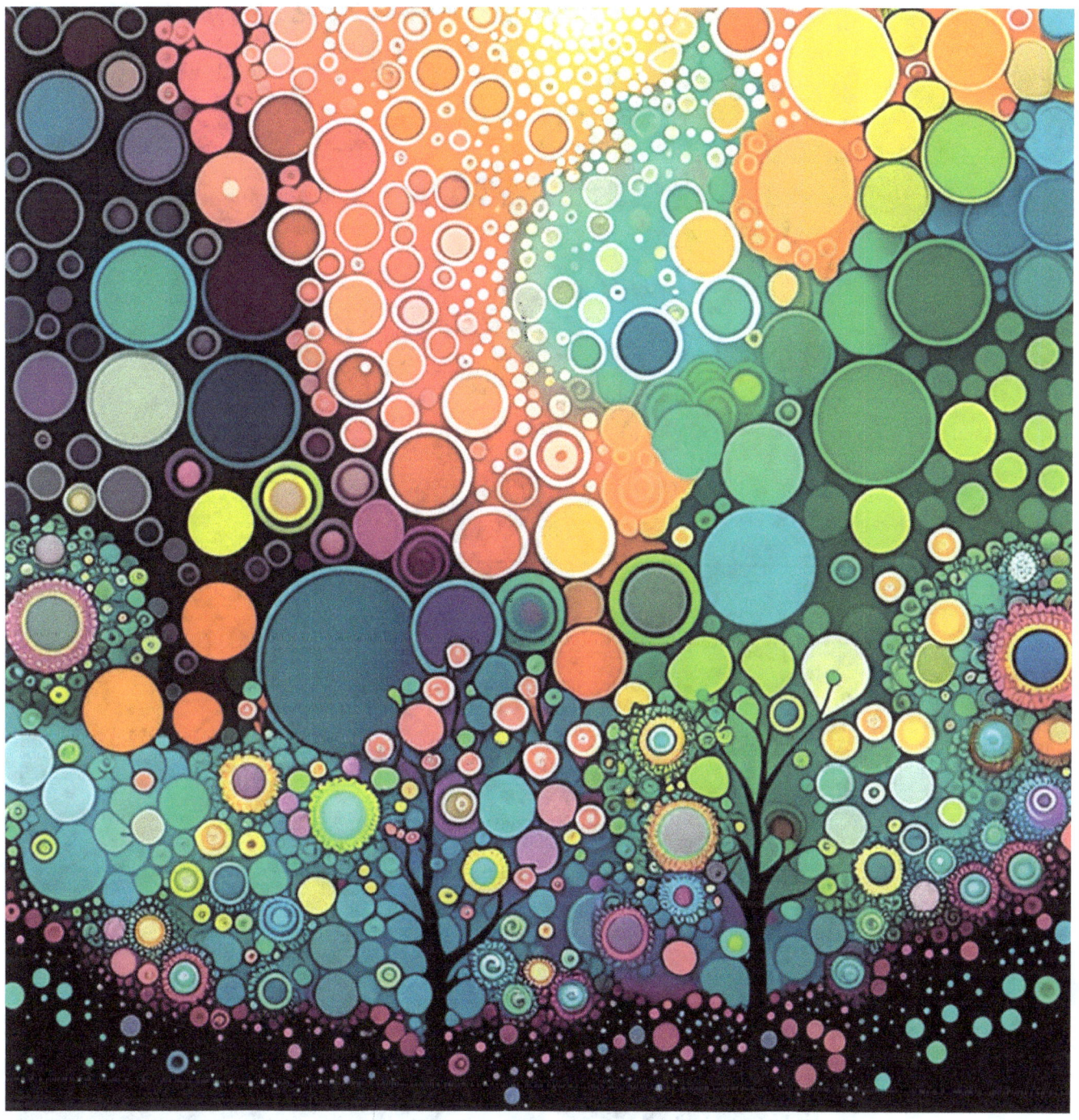

Notice the color arrangement and segmentation create a unique pattern that makes sense.
You now know the secret to coloring books.
See how simple it is my friend?

The picture below is your destination. An EXPERT you are!
Keep this picture in mind as your Reference.

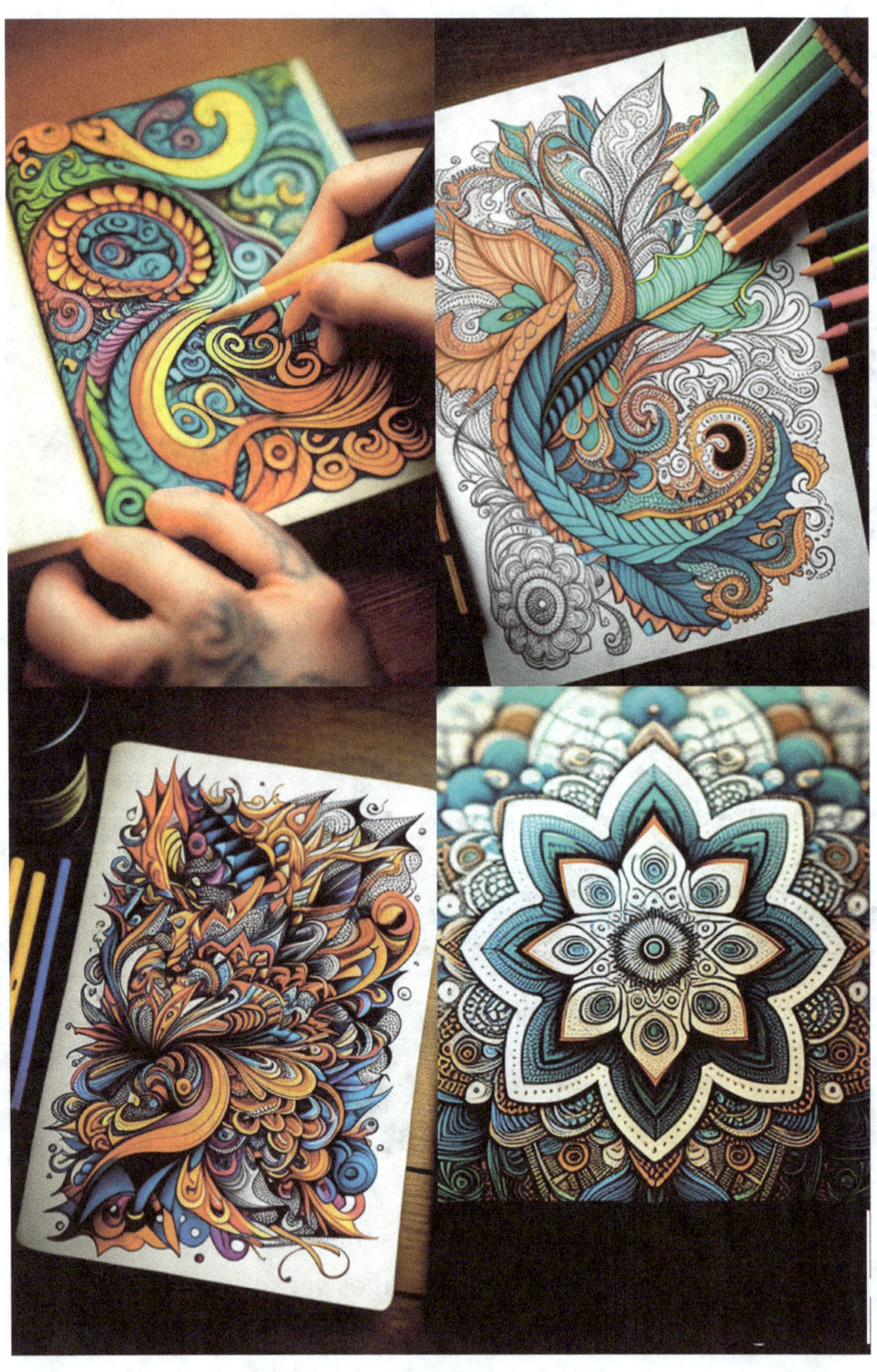

We are in this together, we shall go step-by-step.
AND arrive expertly!

FACT: Plant and flowery patterns are common in coloring books. This is a life-like image to assist you to start, notice the uncolored portion below...

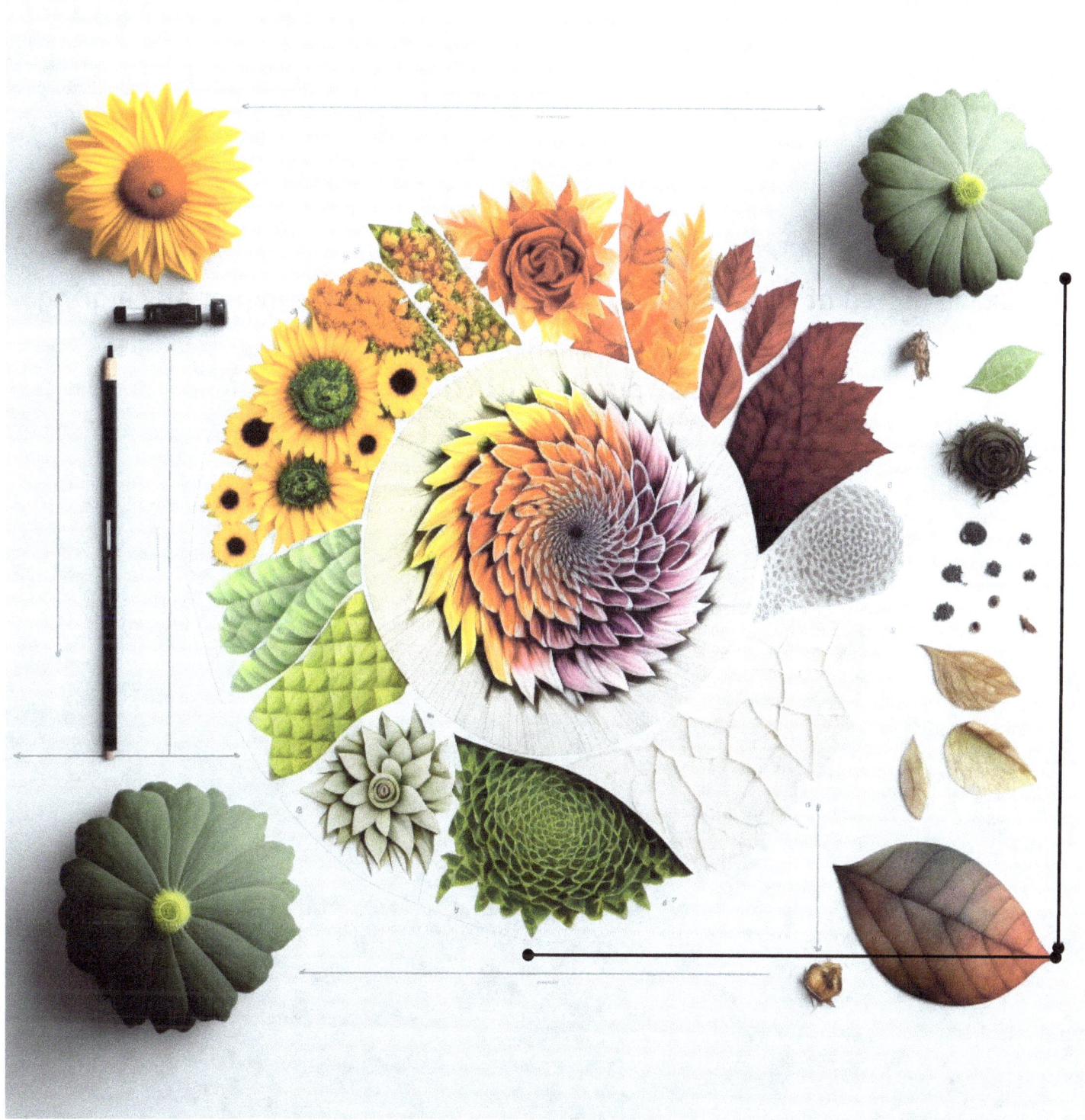

Hint: Using your imagination and the existing color segmentation and arrangement on this image, complete the uncolored portion above...

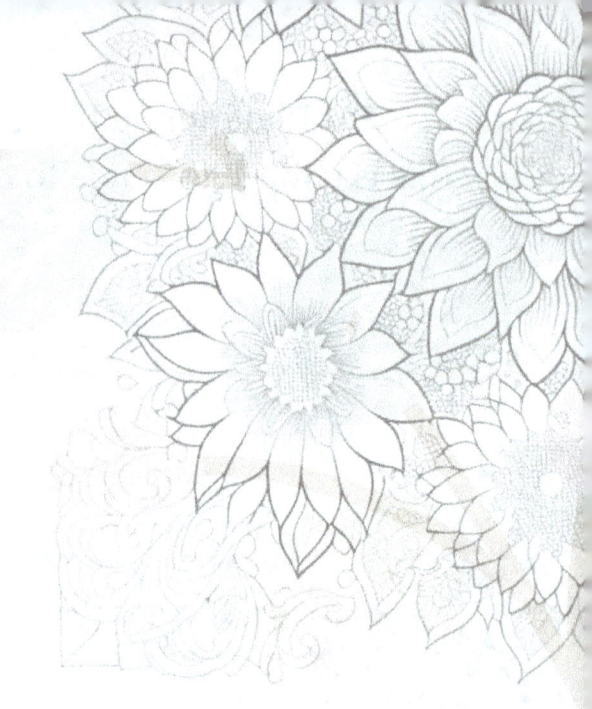

Like we hinted at the start, the first tool, you need to conquer all coloring books...
Is Your IMAGINATION!

Remember that.

GO FOR IT!: Using your imagination and the existing color segmentation and arrangement on this image, complete the uncolored portions below, and add more layers to the already colored portions...

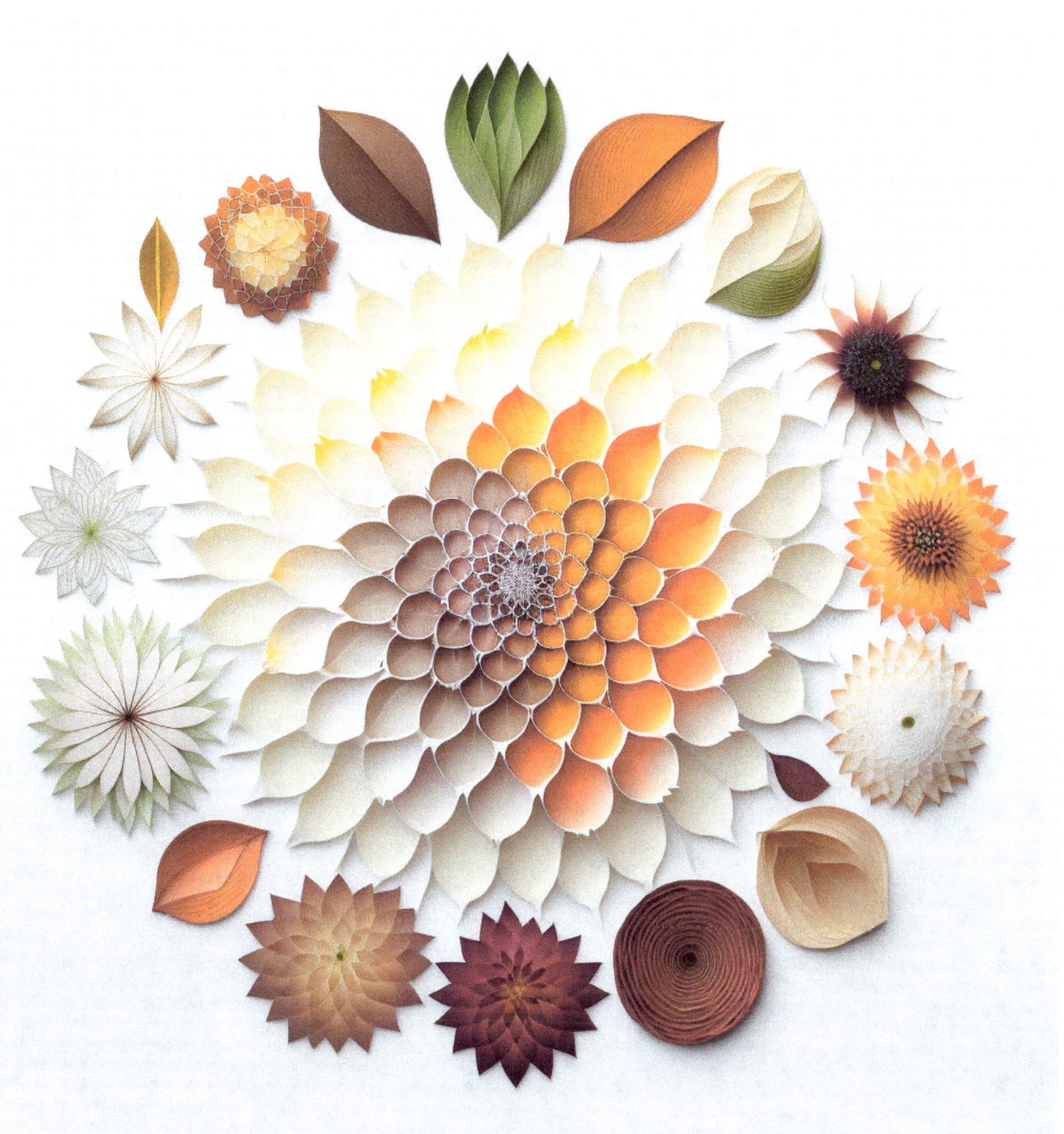

AGAIN!: There are uncolored portions in this image, let us see what you can do with them.

You may choose to use our color hints...

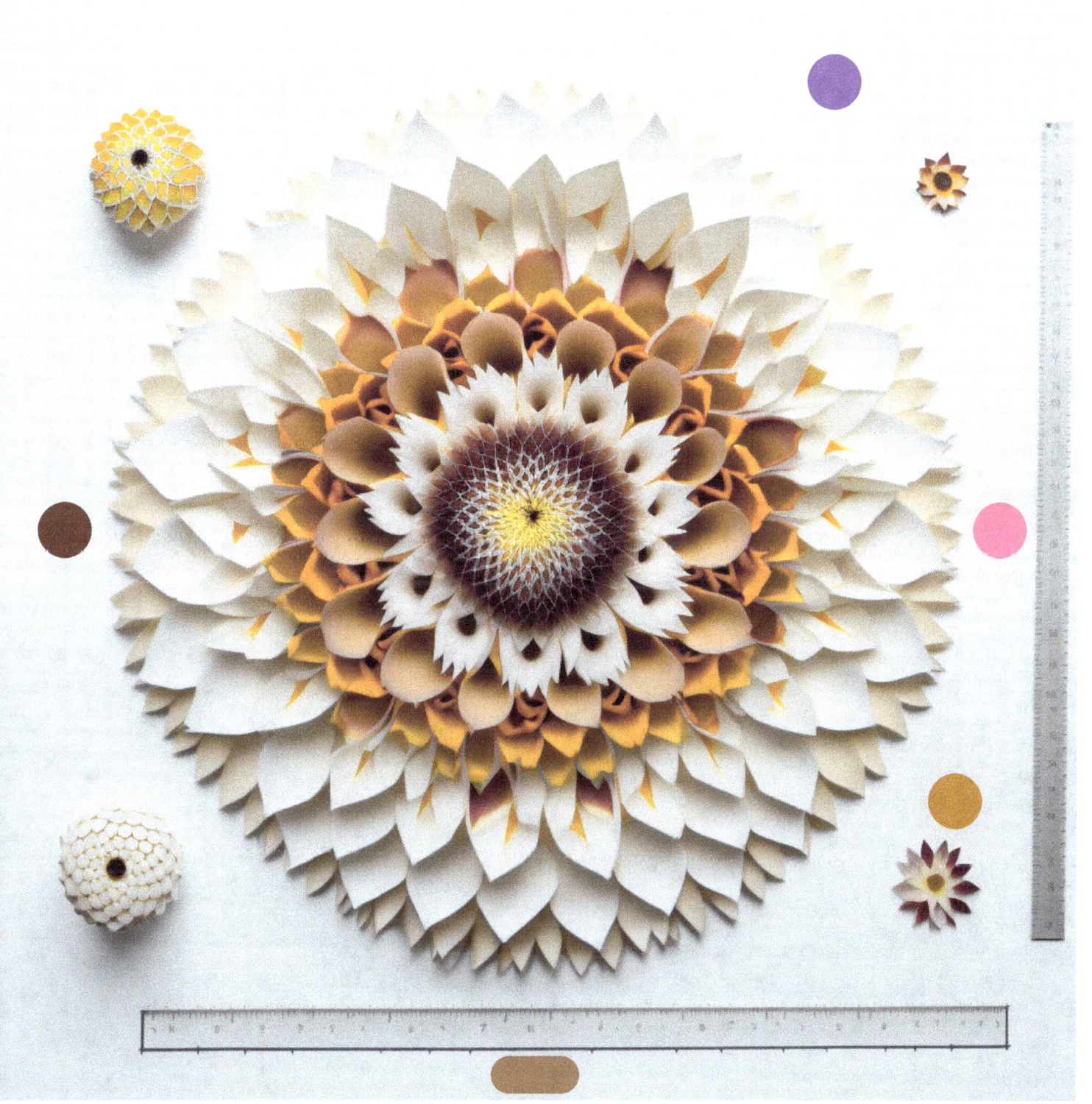

OK, let us switch things up a little, here is another pattern. However, we are nice people so we left a color code guide at the bottom of the image, use it to complete the uncolored portions below...

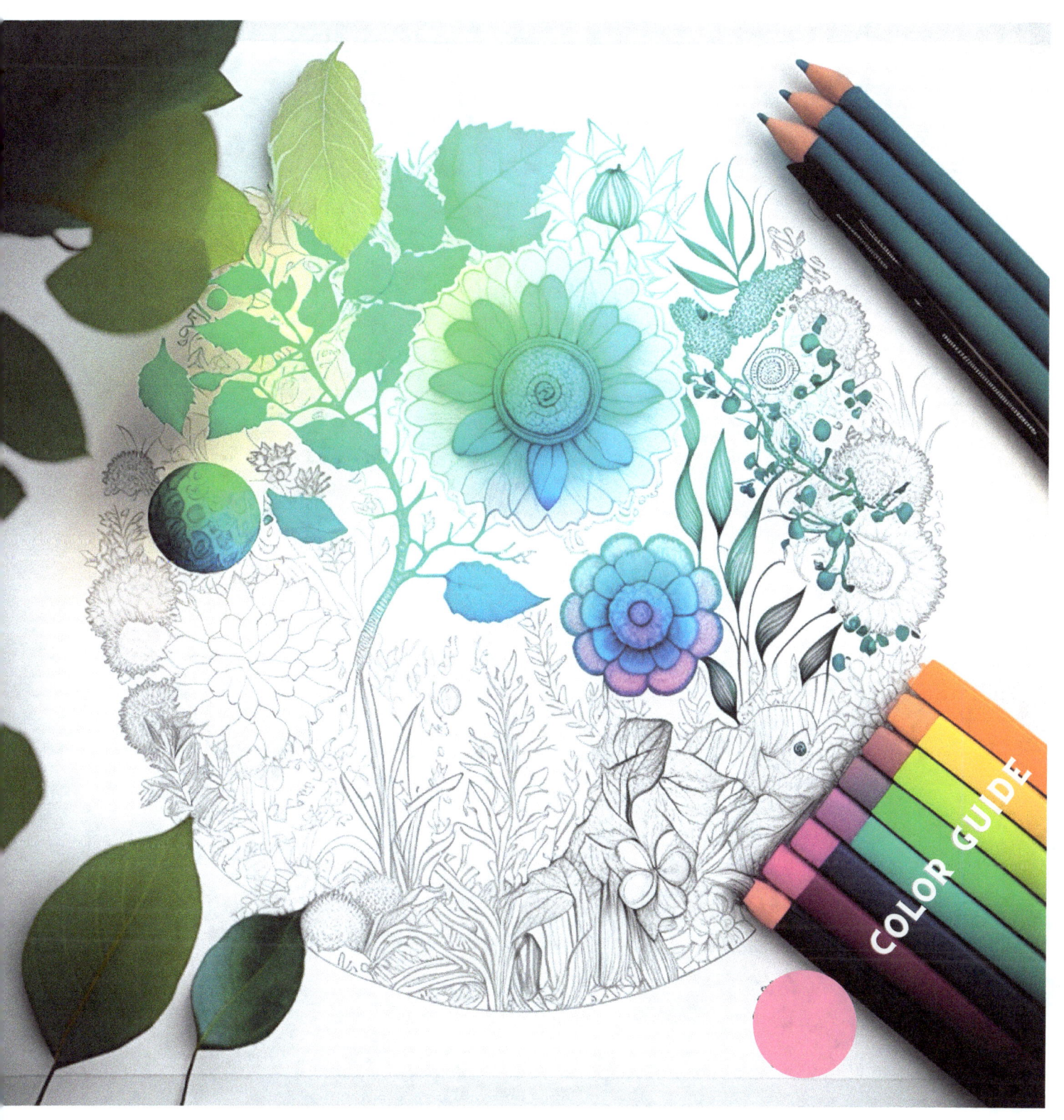

Congratulations! We just arrived in a new CITY!
We are making good progress.
You have done well.

———————●◆●———————

Nature and animals have a good impact on our lives.
This is why they are often used in Art therapy to promote calm and relaxation.

Study the image below.

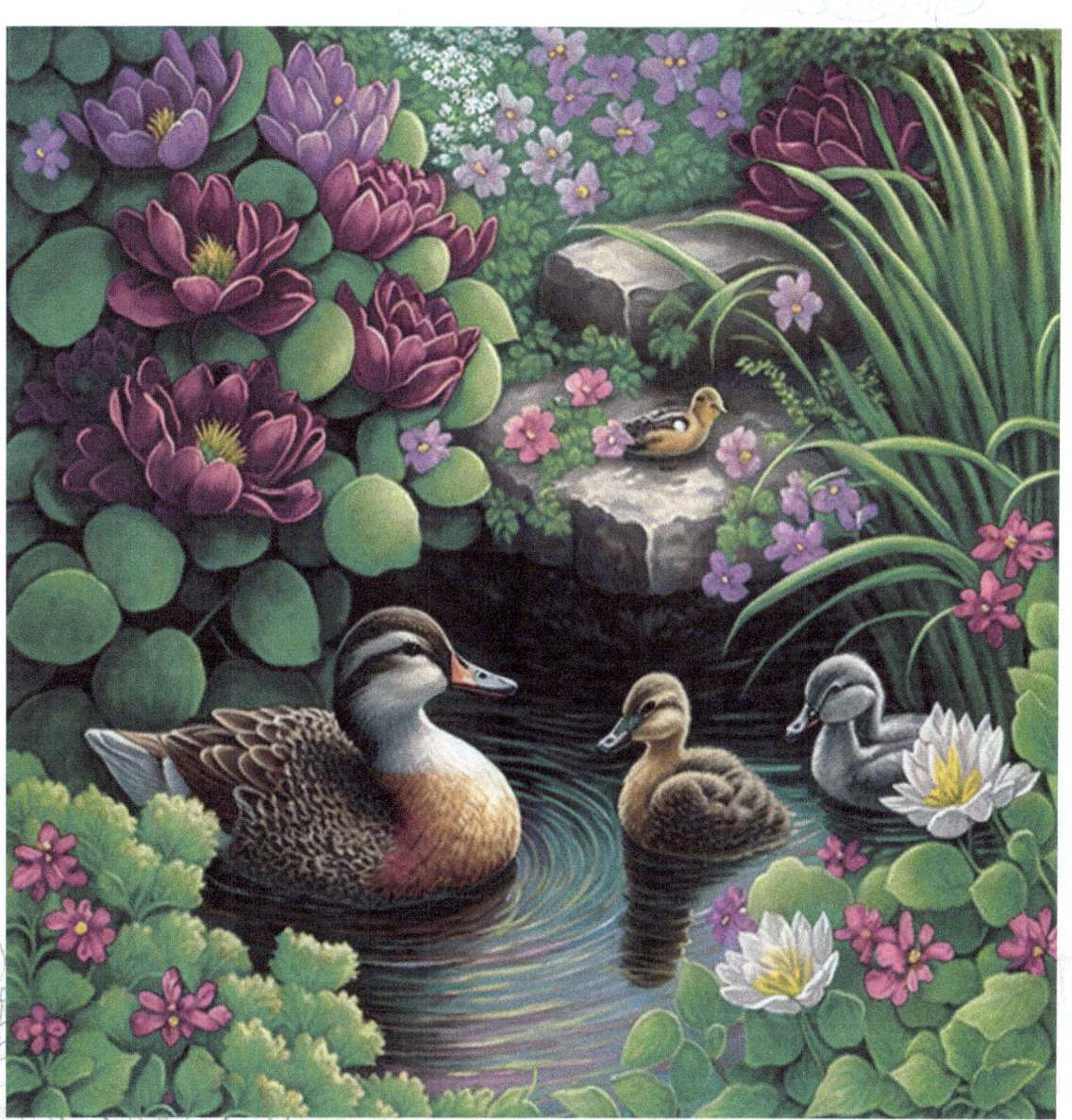

In this new city, we are going to explore its natural scenery,
and how to color its animals.

Heads up!
This is to notify you that, we shall soon have to let you drive all by yourself.

Study the reference images below.

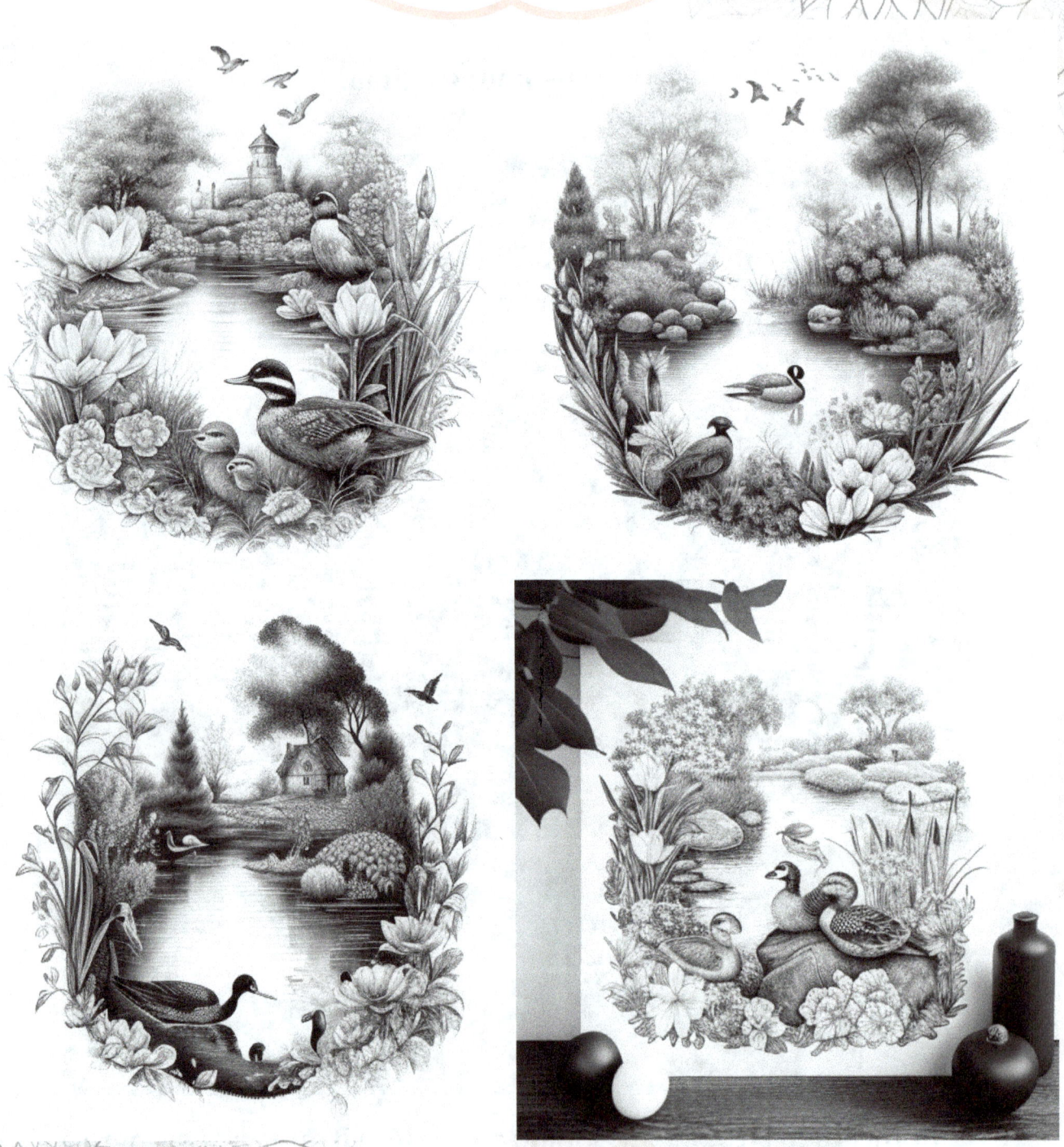

We believe in you that you got this,
so we shall introduce these types of images and patterns in full force soon!

Remember the color arrangement and segmentation you memorized
at the start of our journey?
You need it now.

Go ahead, use the color code guide at the bottom, and complete the portions below.

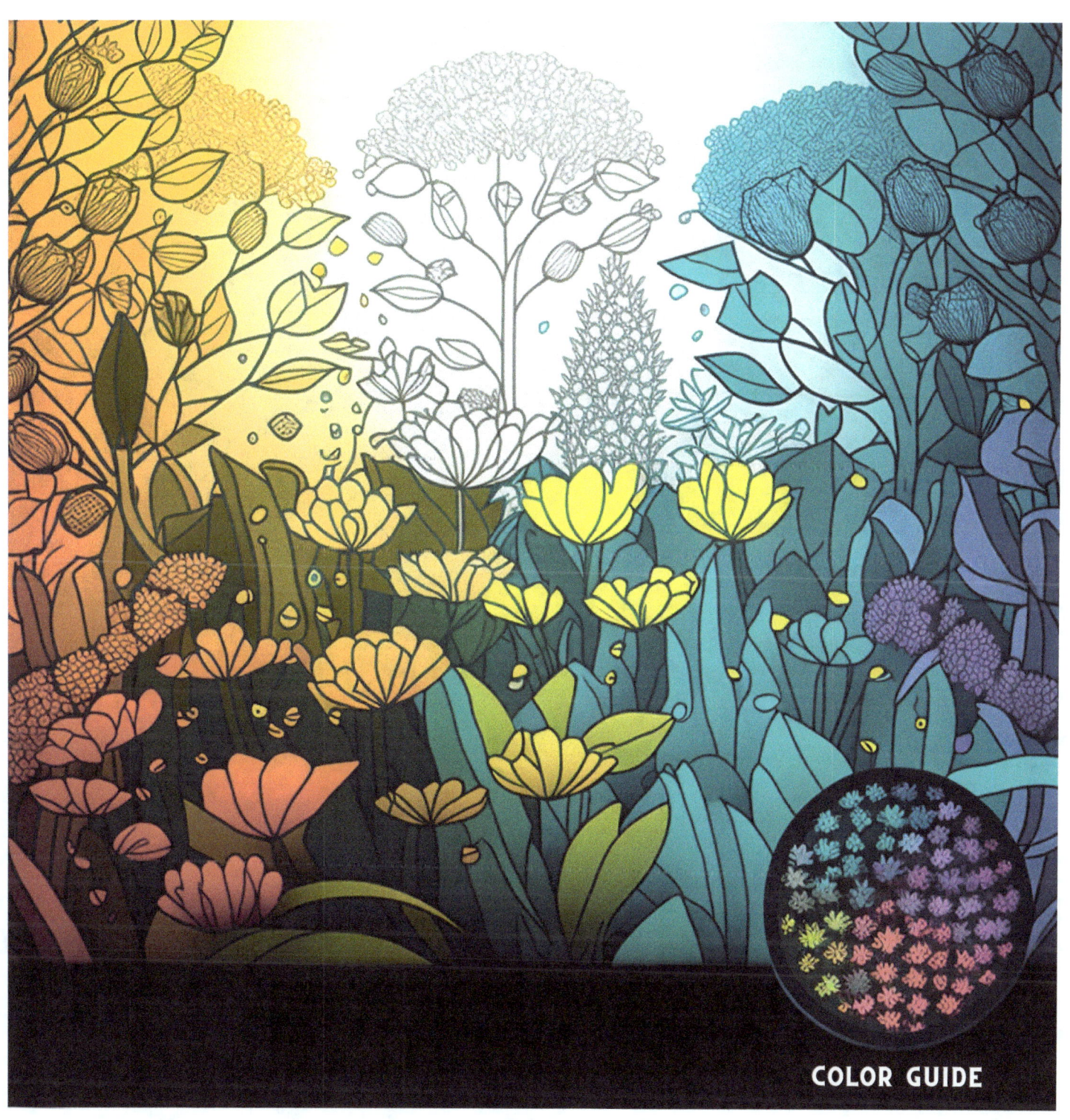

COLOR GUIDE

You just finished coloring beautiful scenery.
Animals often appear in different sceneries, so you need to learn how to color animals.
Go ahead, use the color code guide on the right, and complete coloring the cute Owl.

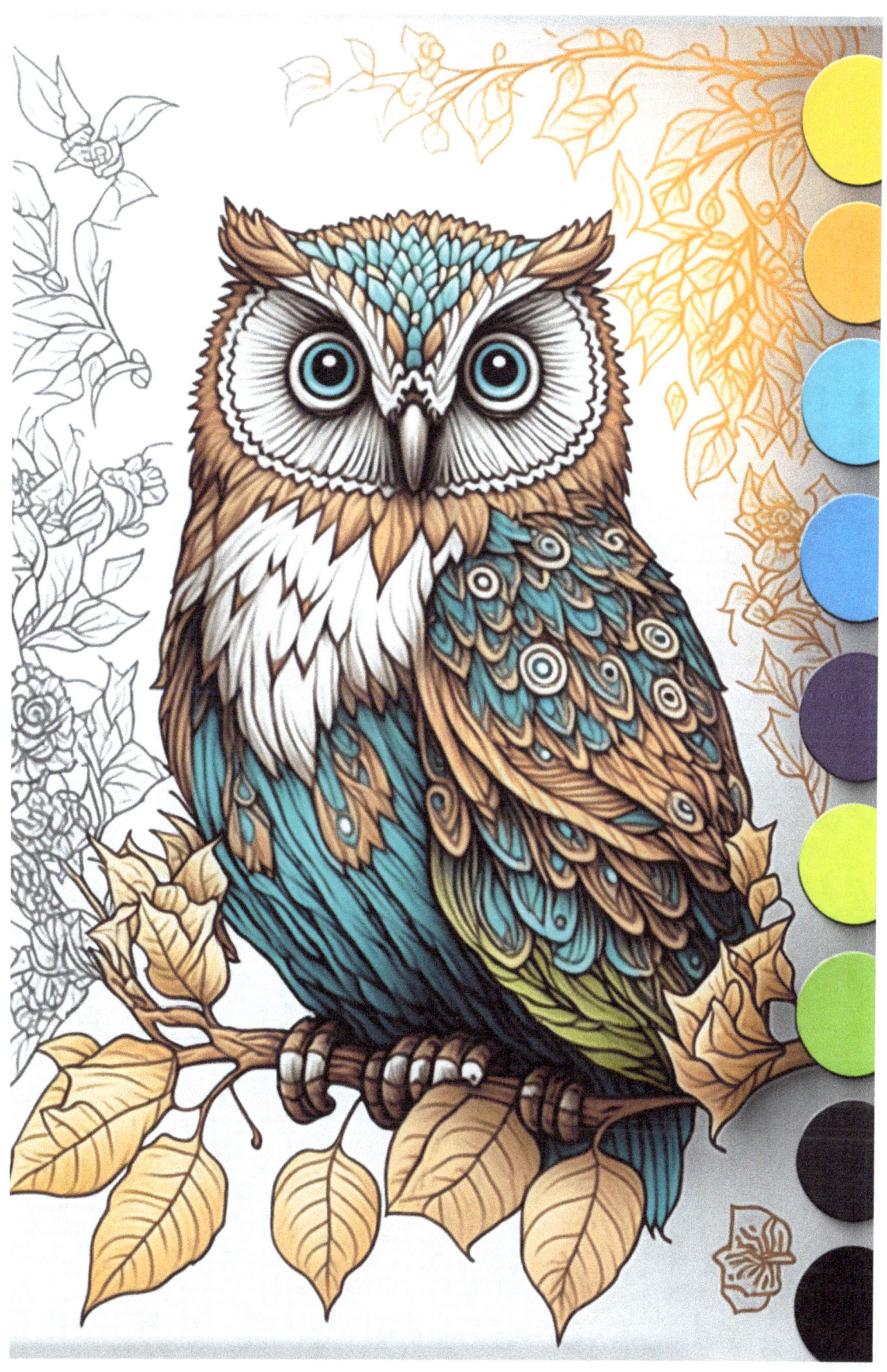

You just finished coloring a cute Owl.
Here now, color another bird, a Parrot.

We believe you are better at it now, so no more color code guides from here onwards.
You definitely got this. Enjoy!

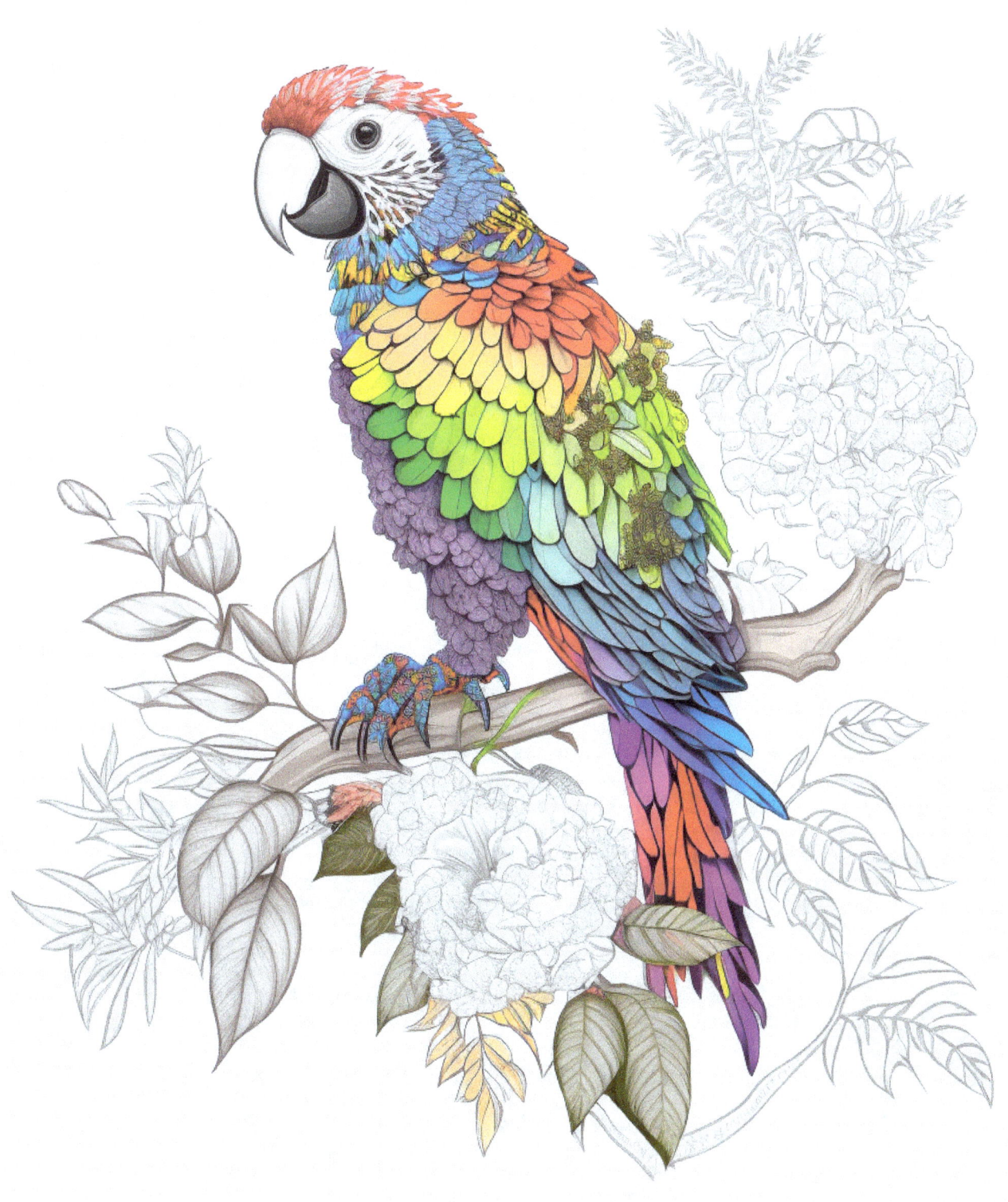

Hello, Expert!

How is it going?

───────•◆•───────

It is time for you to take over this journey.
Use your IMAGINATION and journey everywhere with colors we have not
shown or introduced to you.

Enjoy the ride!

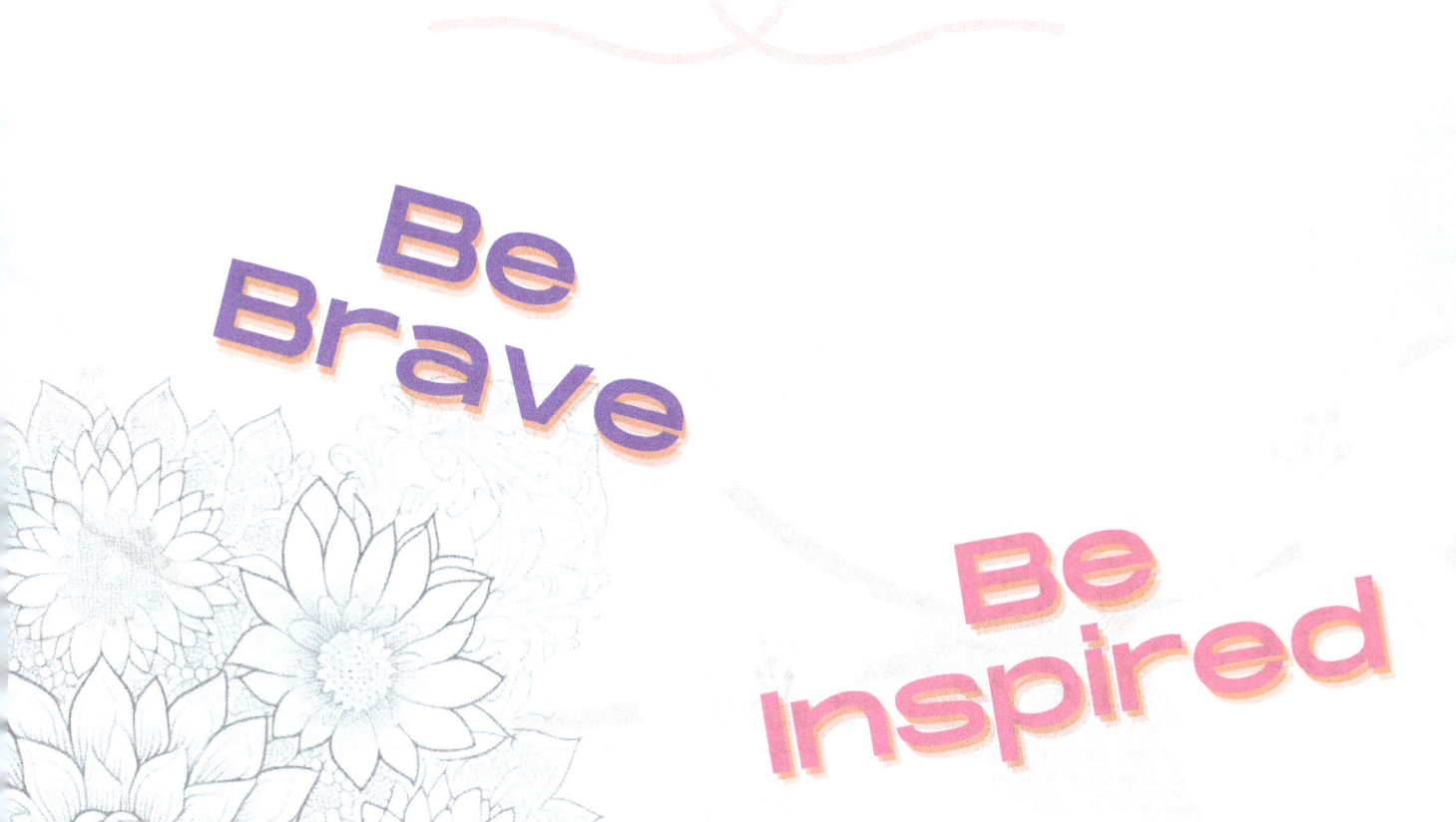

Be
Brave

Be
Inspired

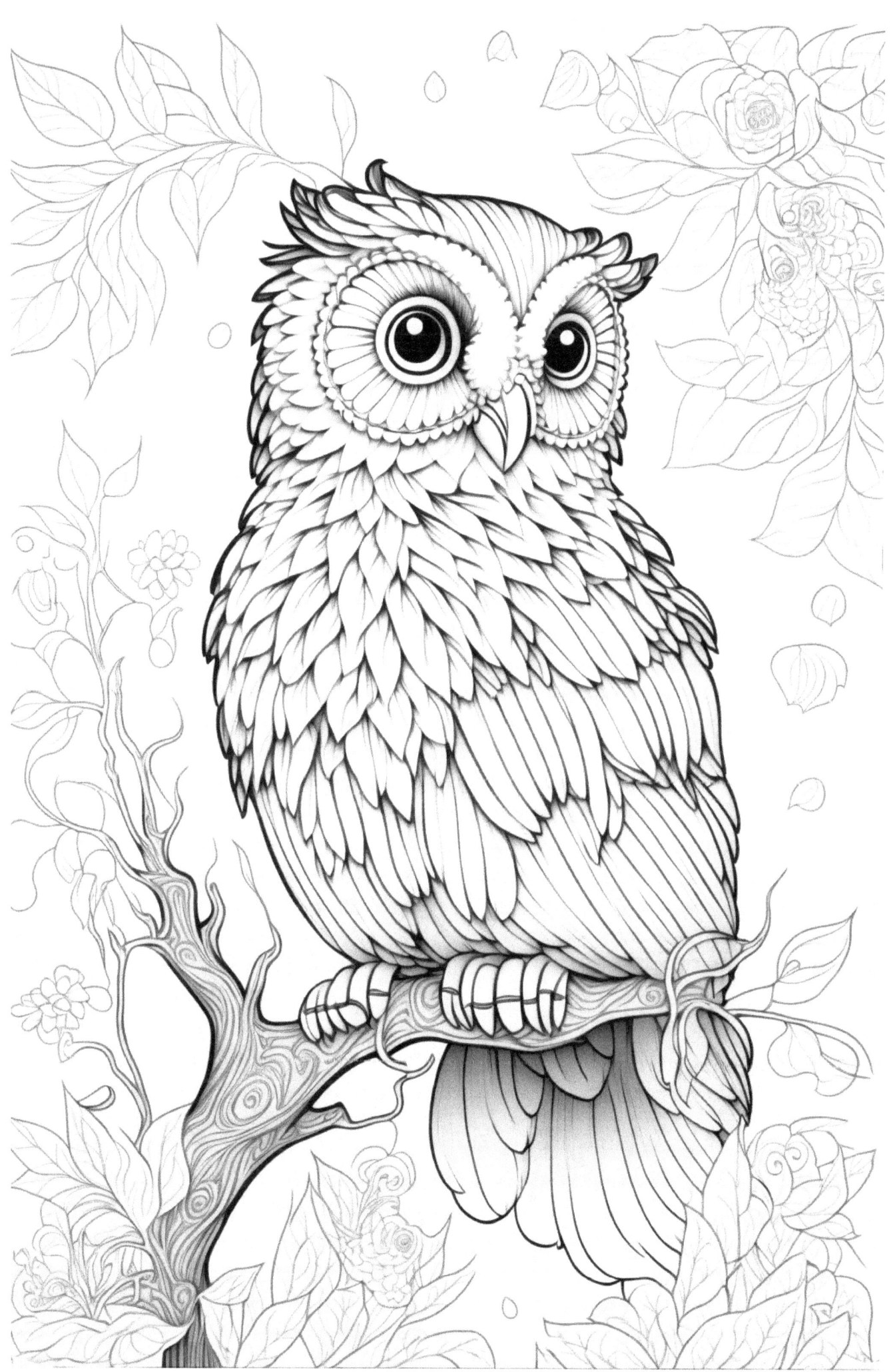

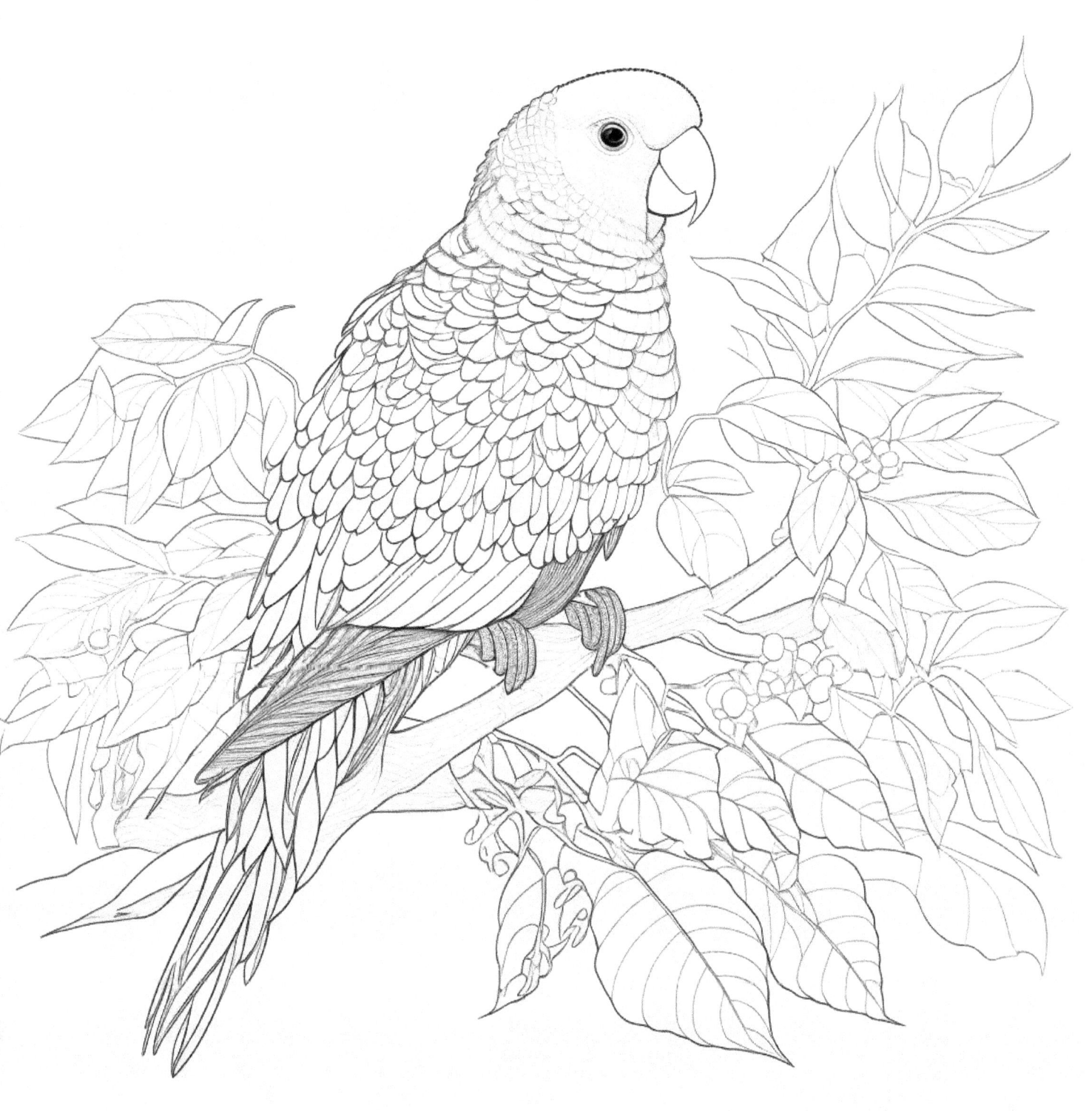

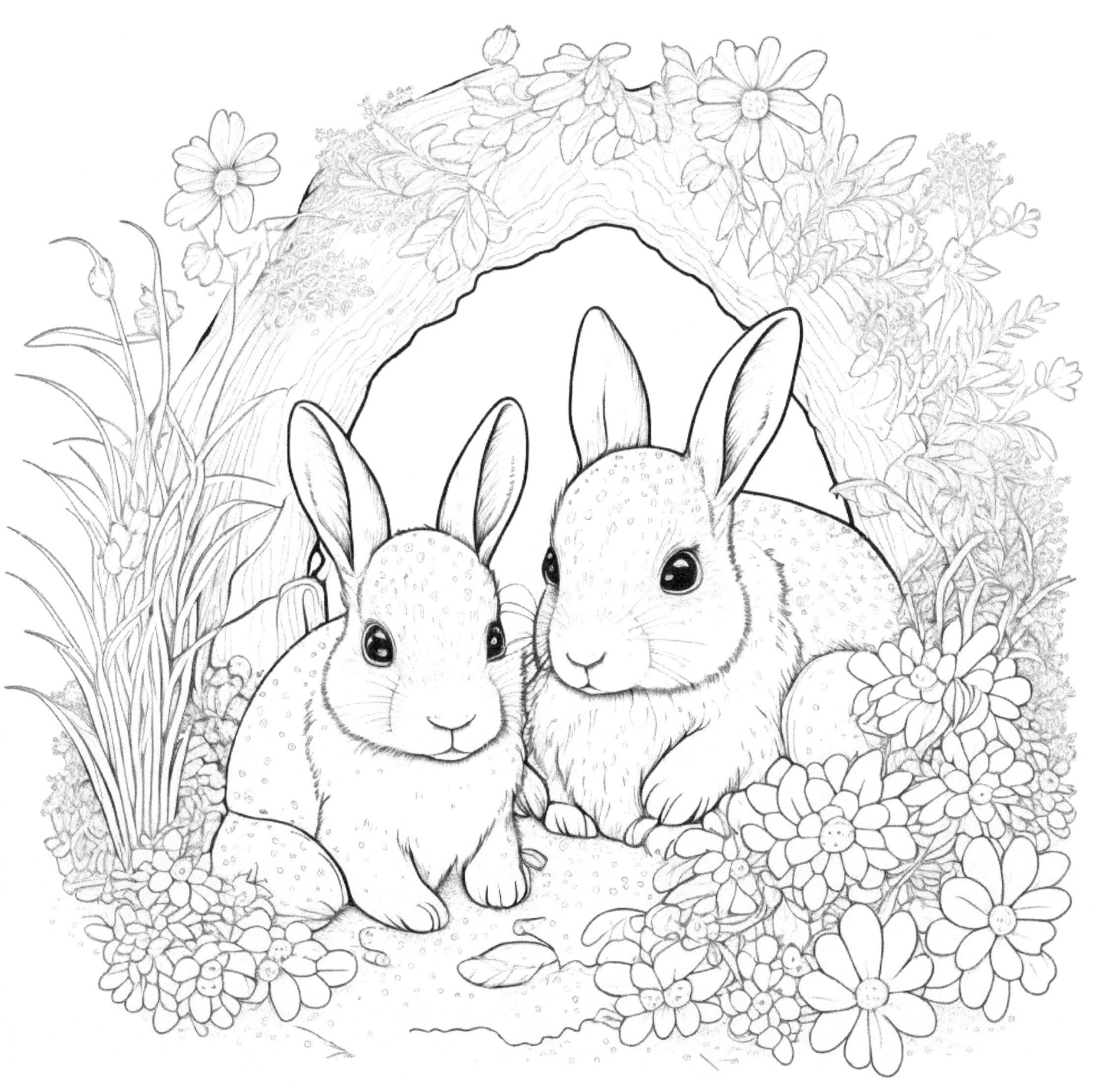

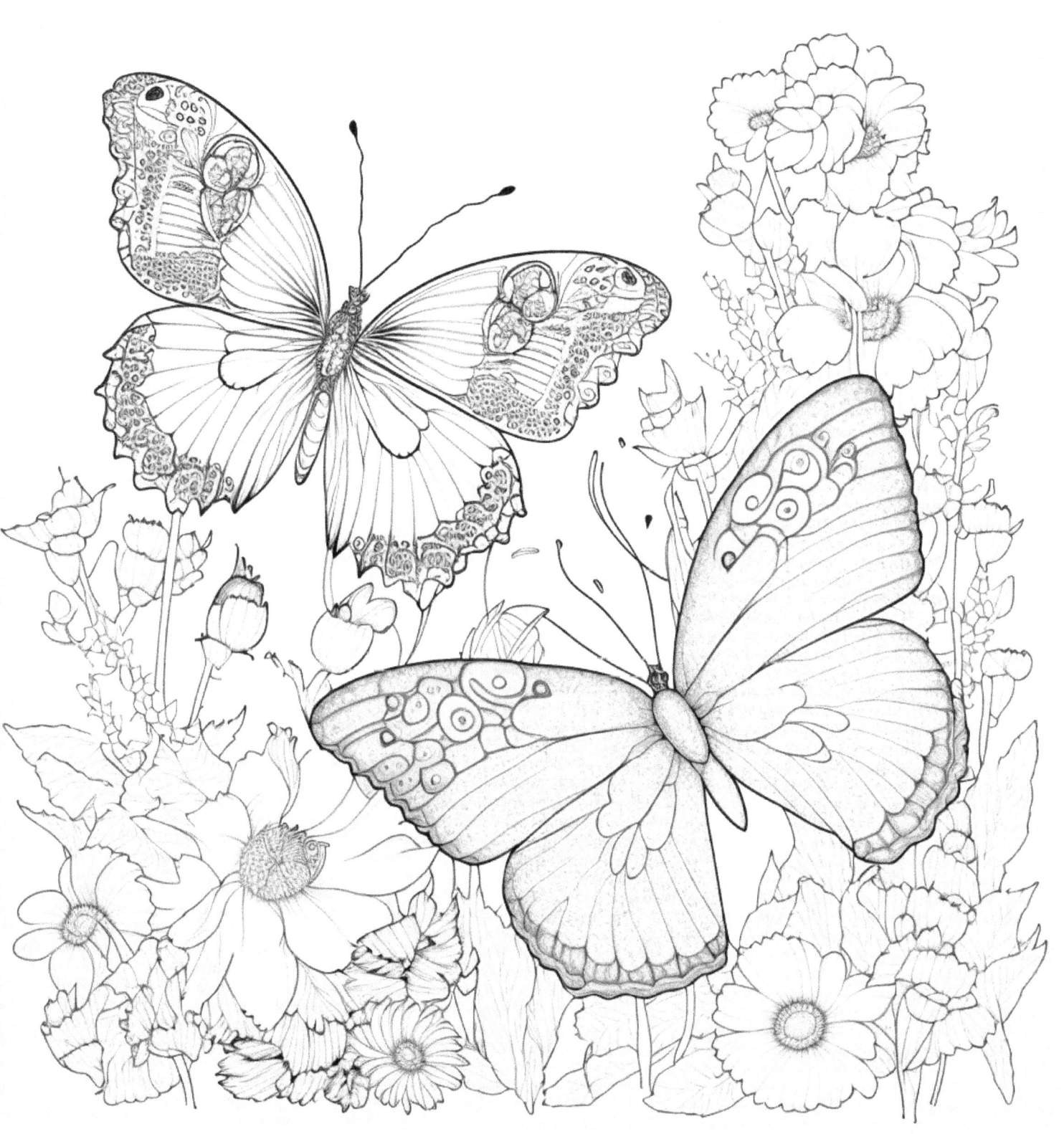

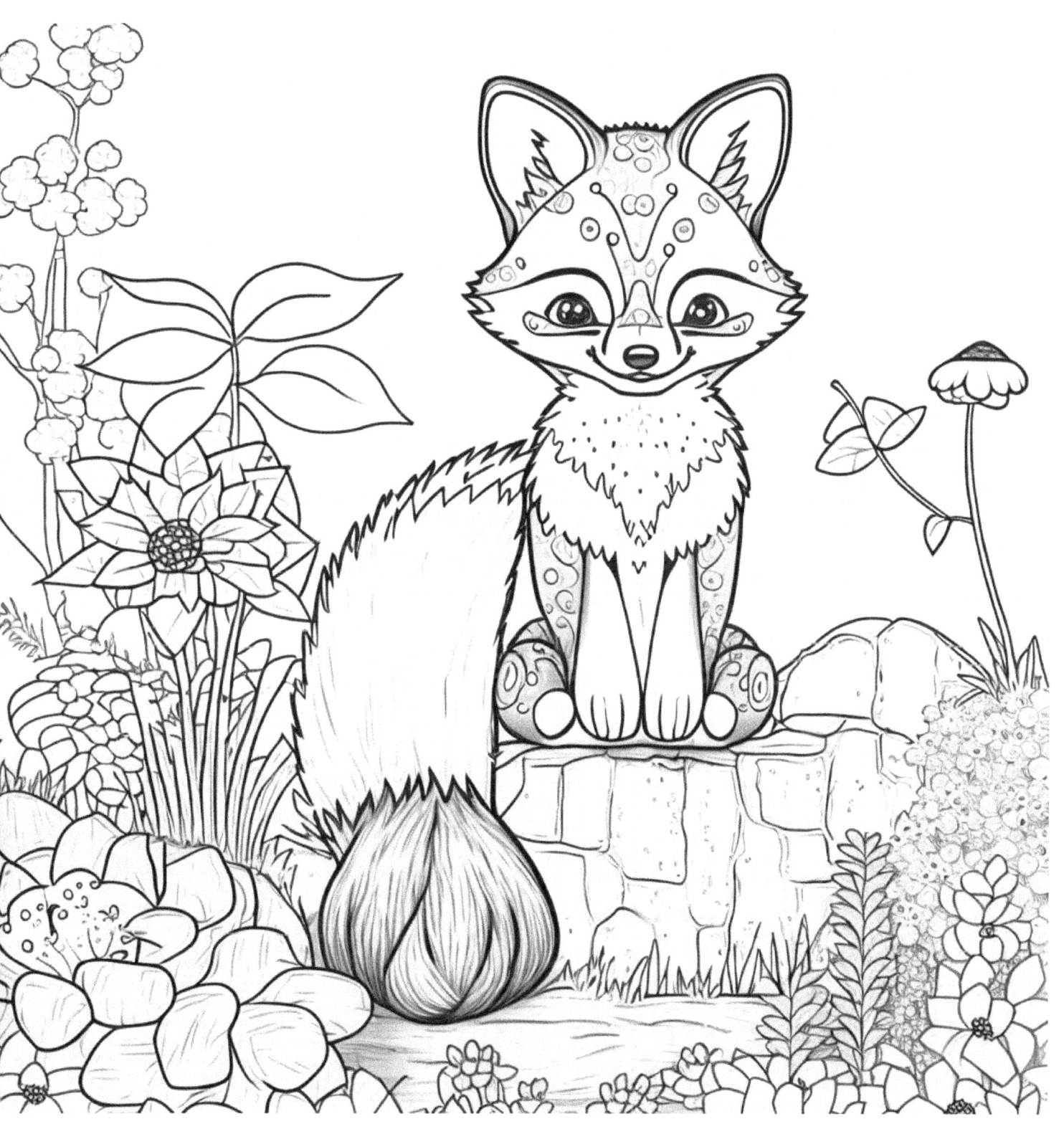

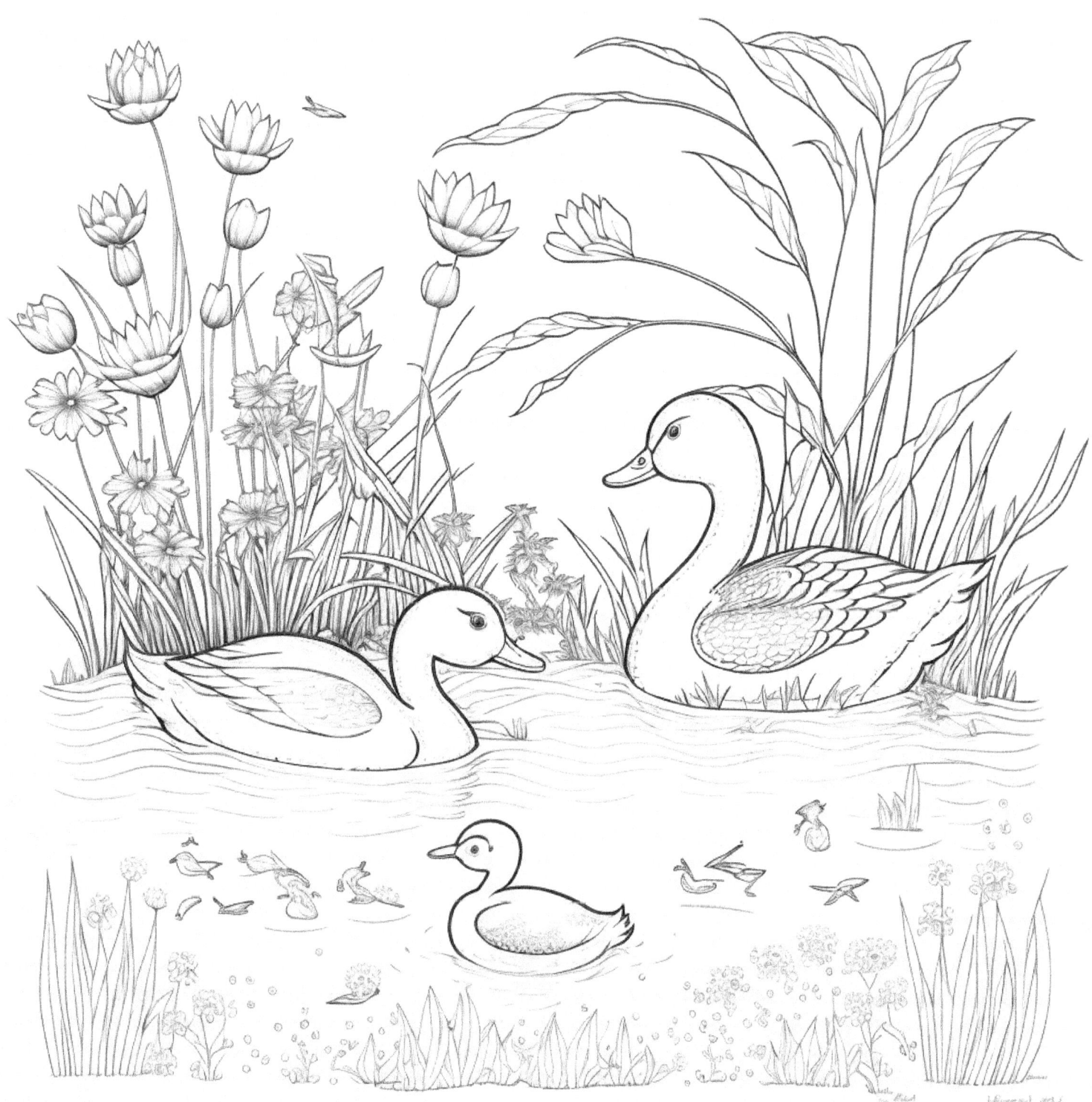

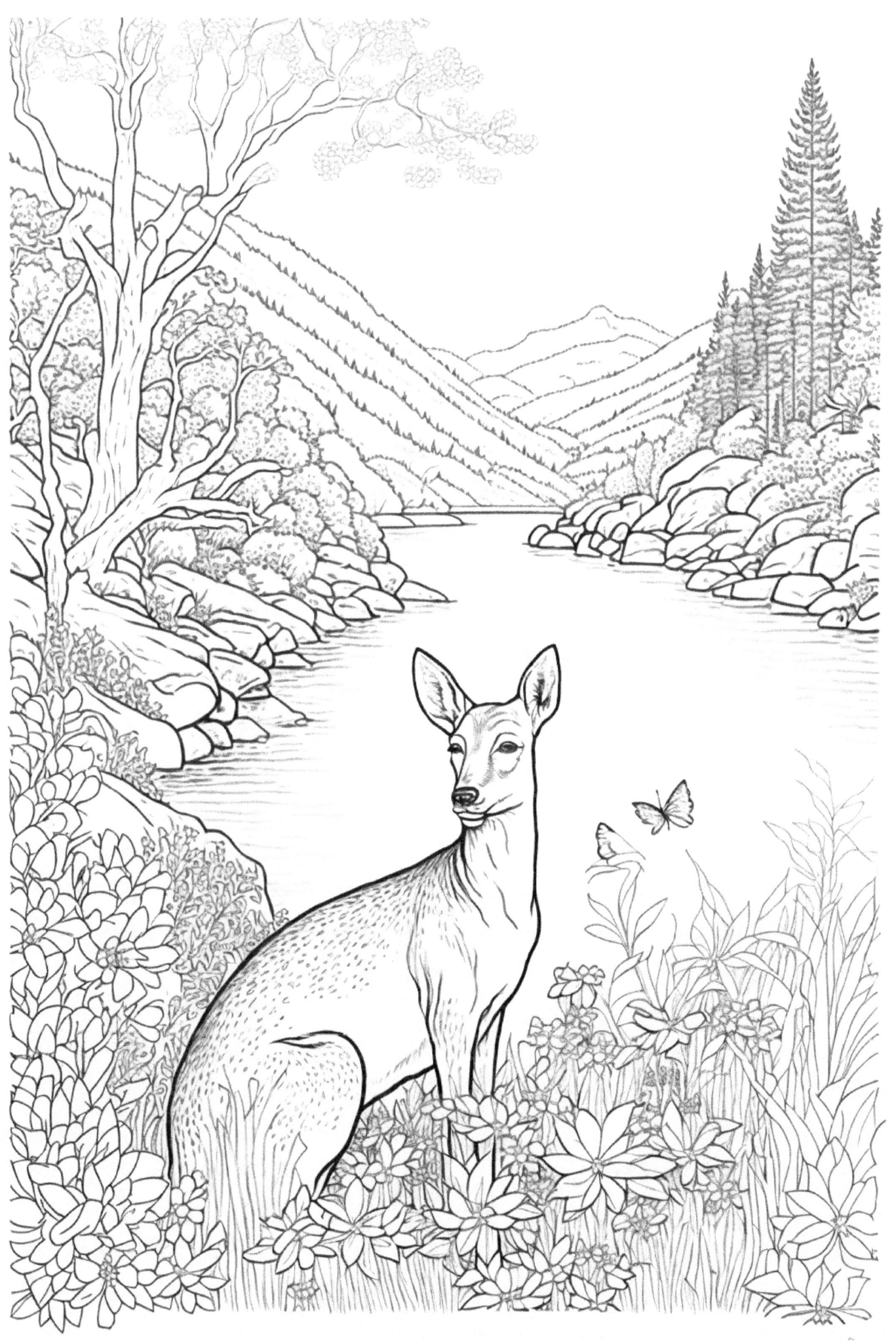

It's time to challenge our Expert!

We have arrived safely at the CITY of "Deep Intricate Designs and Patterns!"

It is time to go further, and journey deeper.

Use your power of FOCUS and IMAGINATION!

.

Off you go!

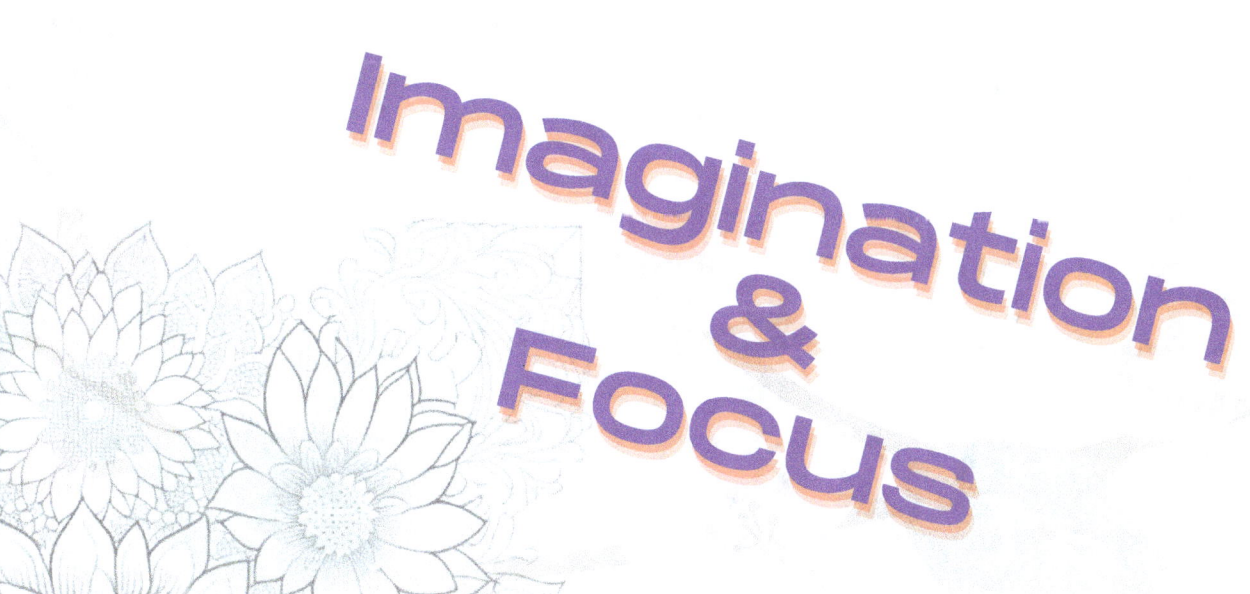

FACT: Animals too can be colored with intricate color strokes.

The donkey below has been colored with light strokes, add your own color strokes on the existing coloring to make it darker, and finish coloring the uncolored portions like the Donkey's nose

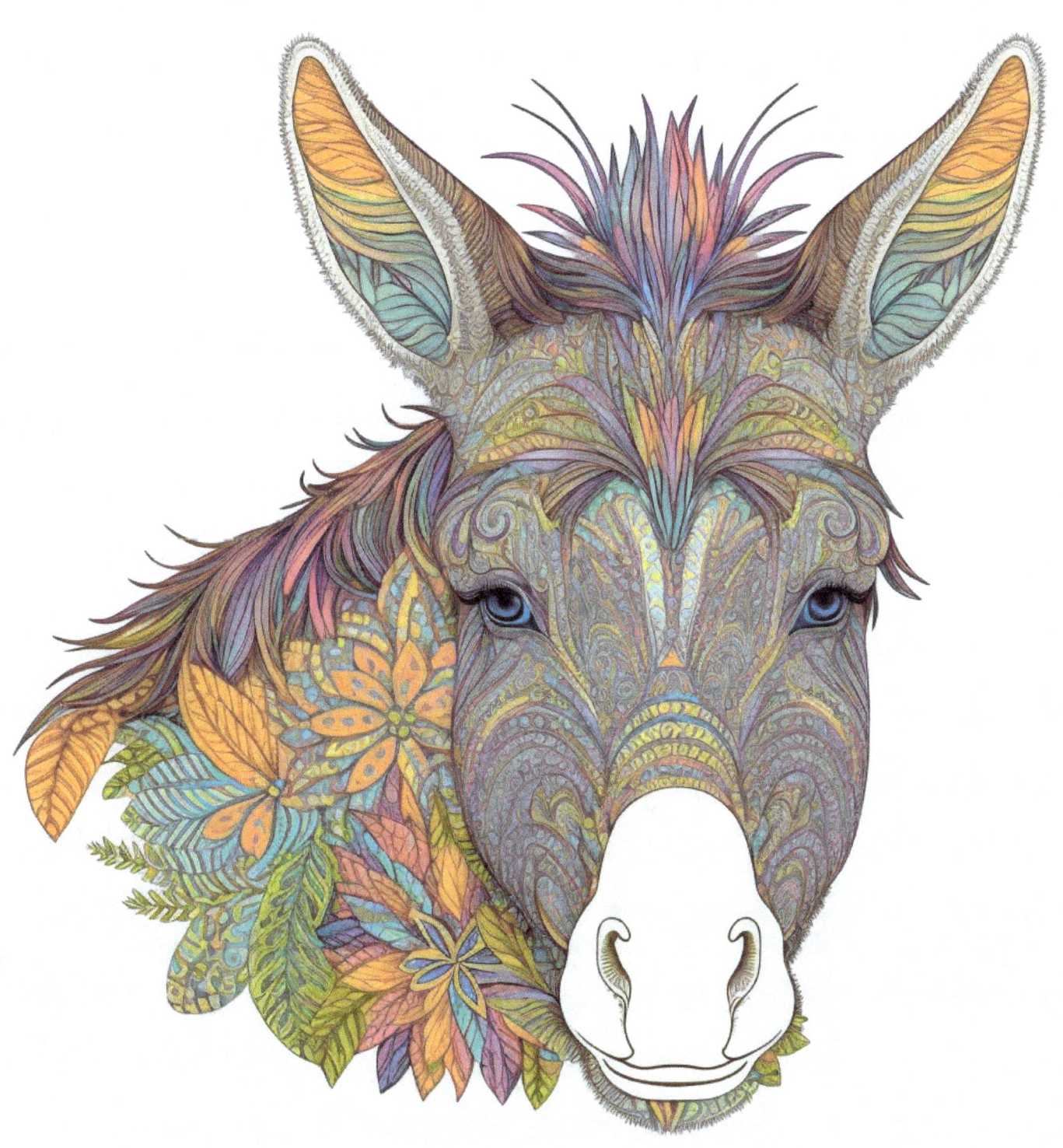

The Deer below has been colored with light strokes, please add your own color strokes on the existing coloring to make it darker, and finish coloring the uncolored portions like the Deer's ears.

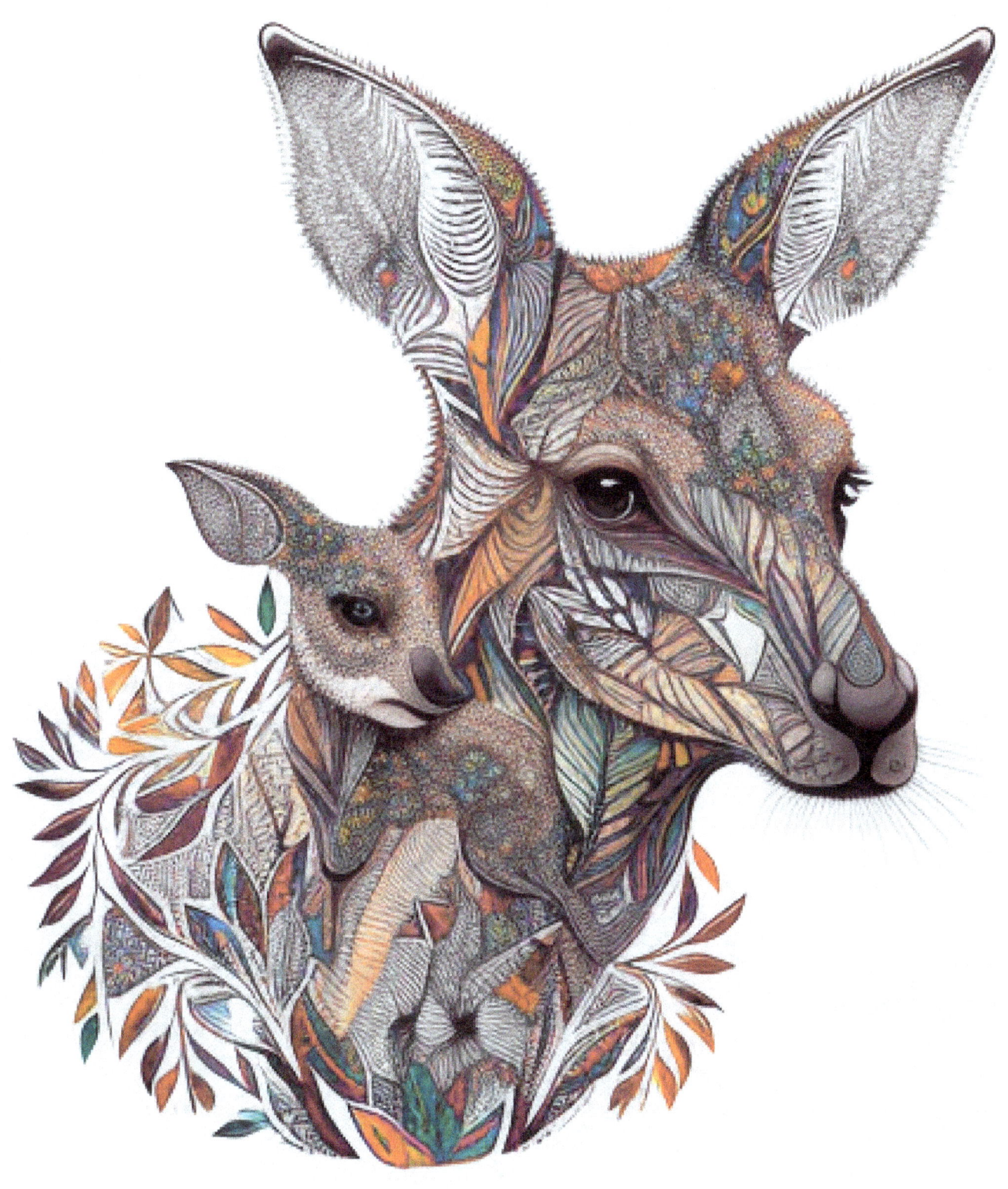

This beautiful Lion needs your make-up, please color it all up!

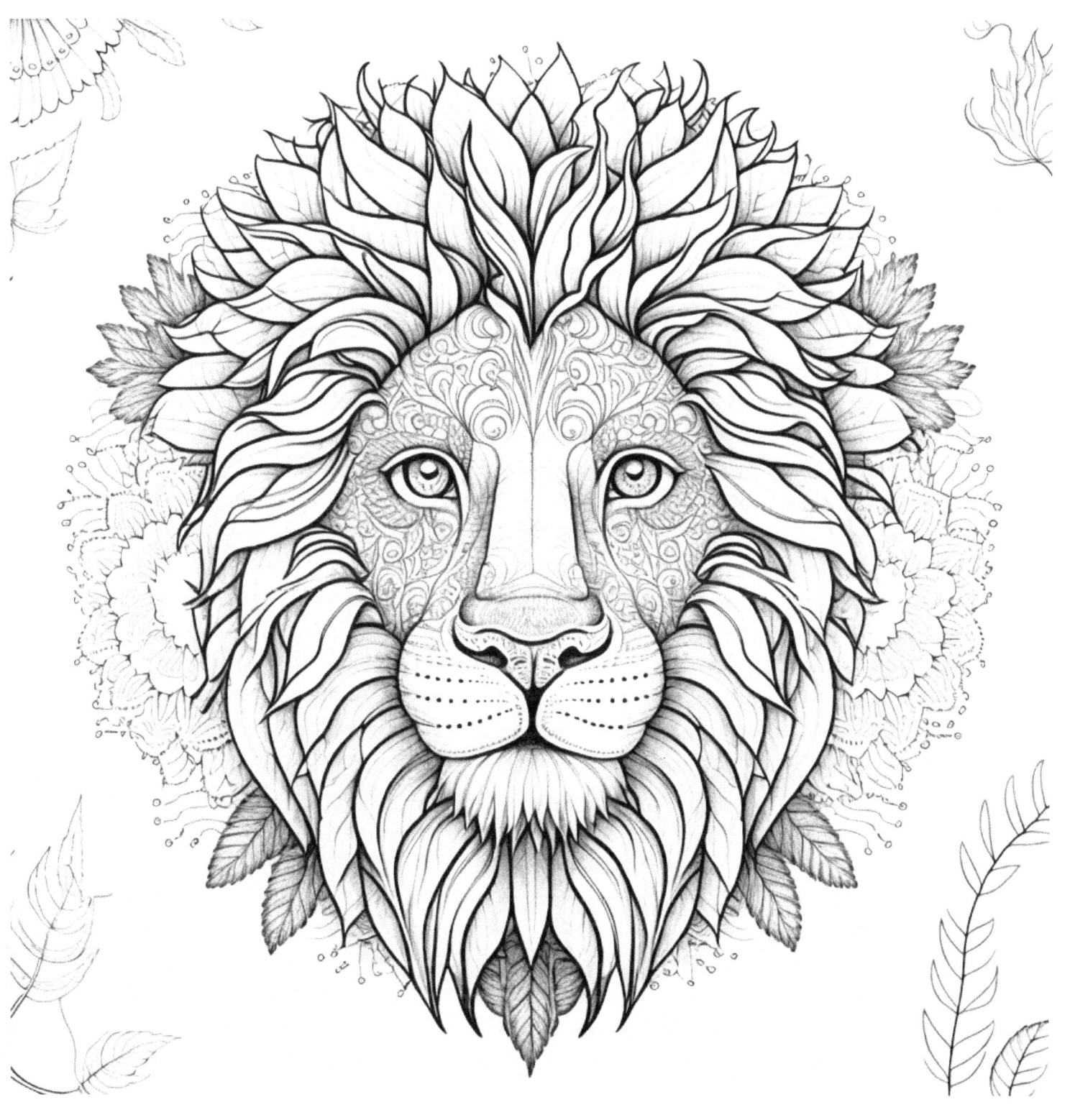

The image below was designed with intricate patterns, to teach you flowery intricate color stroking. Color it all up!

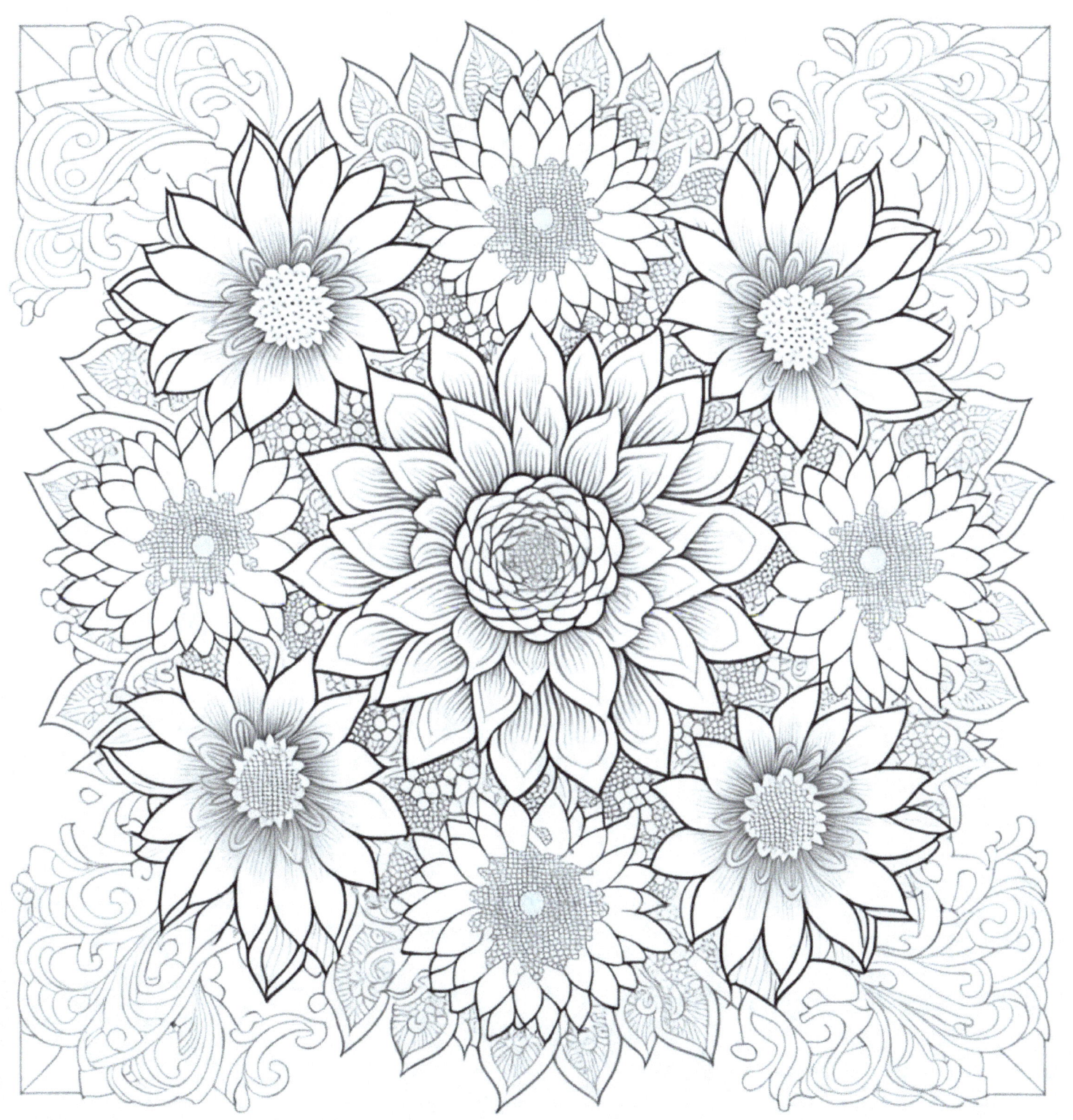

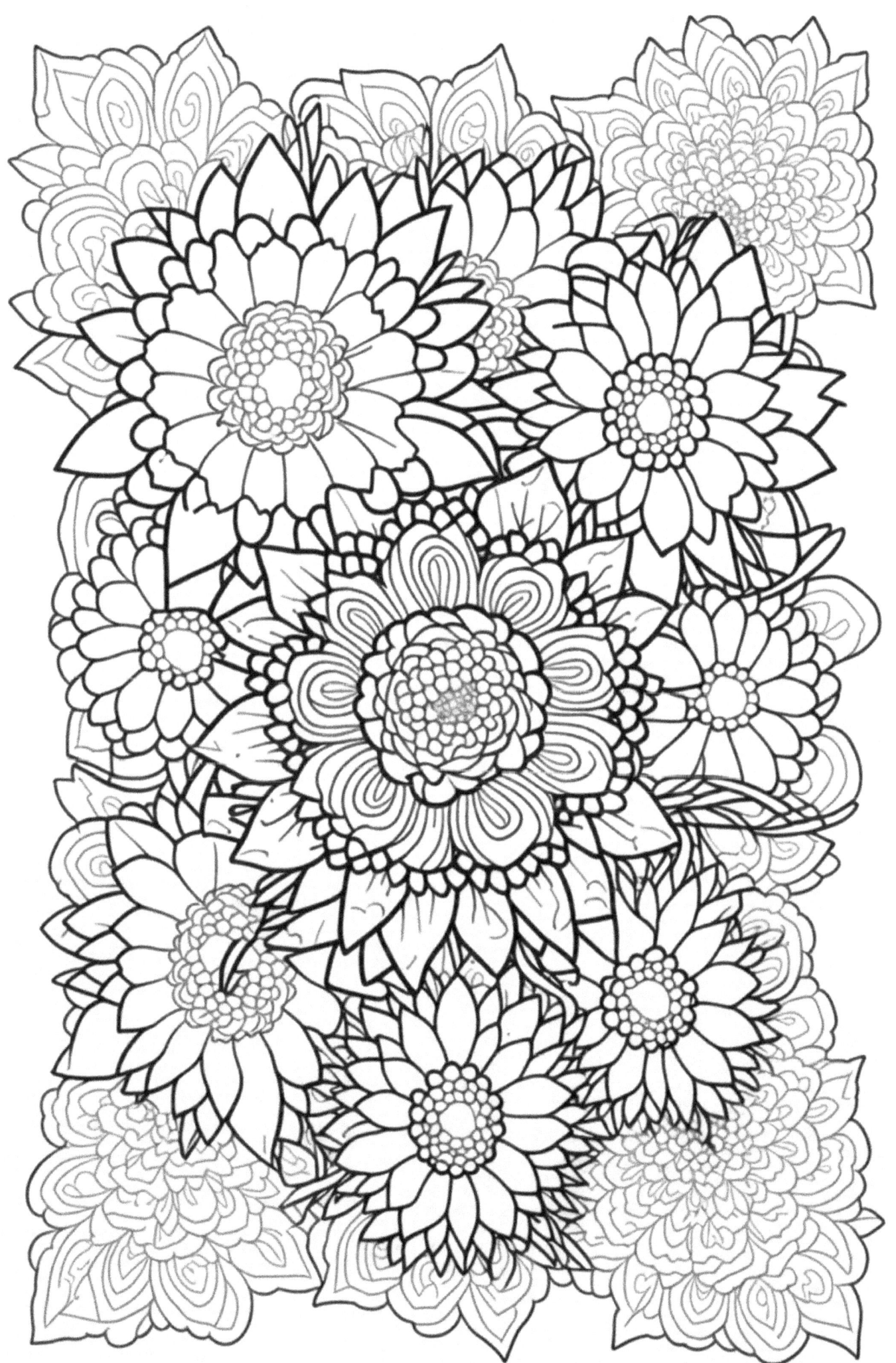

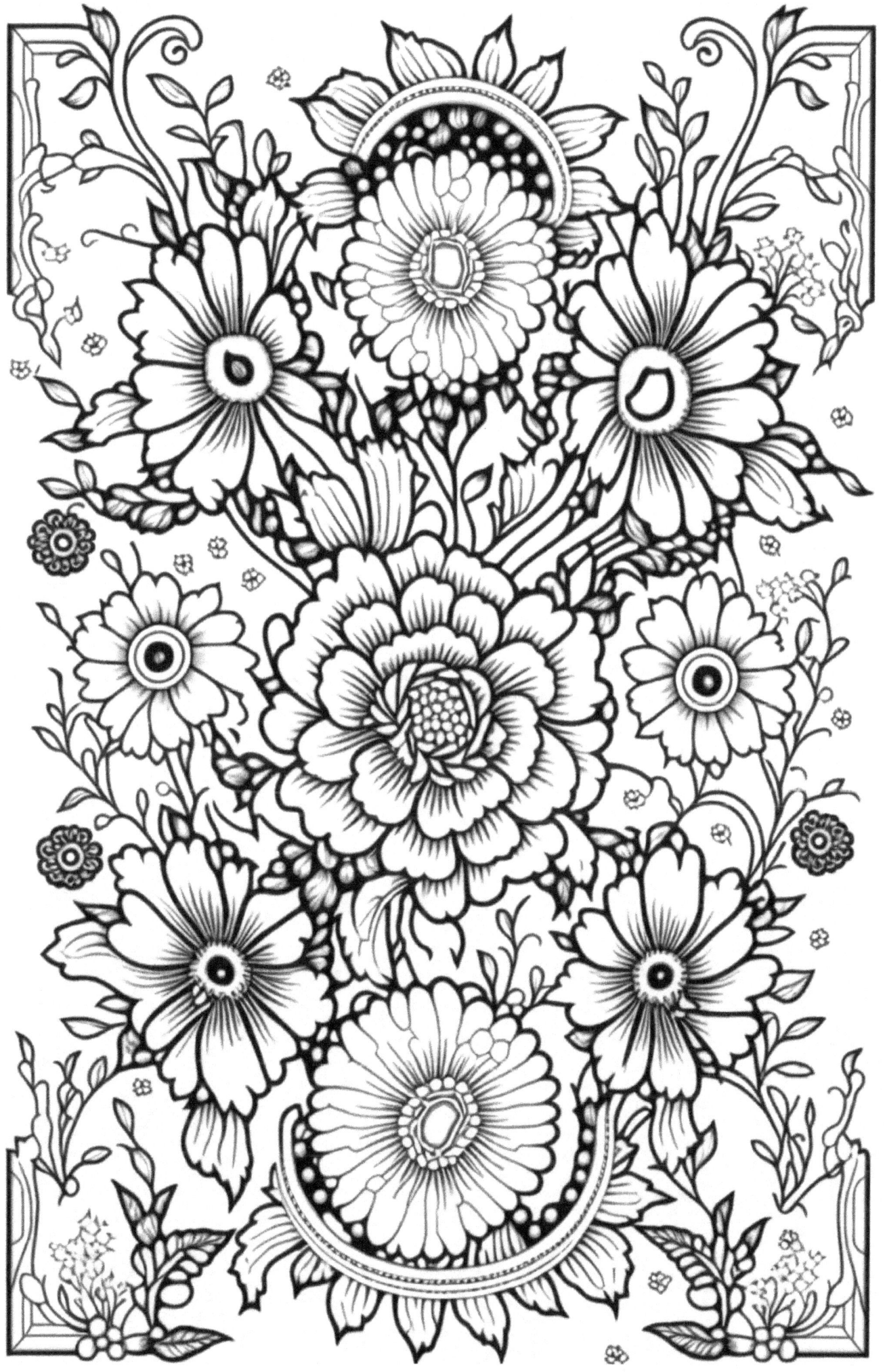

Therapeutic Update!

We have arrived safely at the CITY of "Positivity!"

It is time to take yourself out for a treat!

Give yourself credit, and love yourself, you are valuable!

.

Off you go!

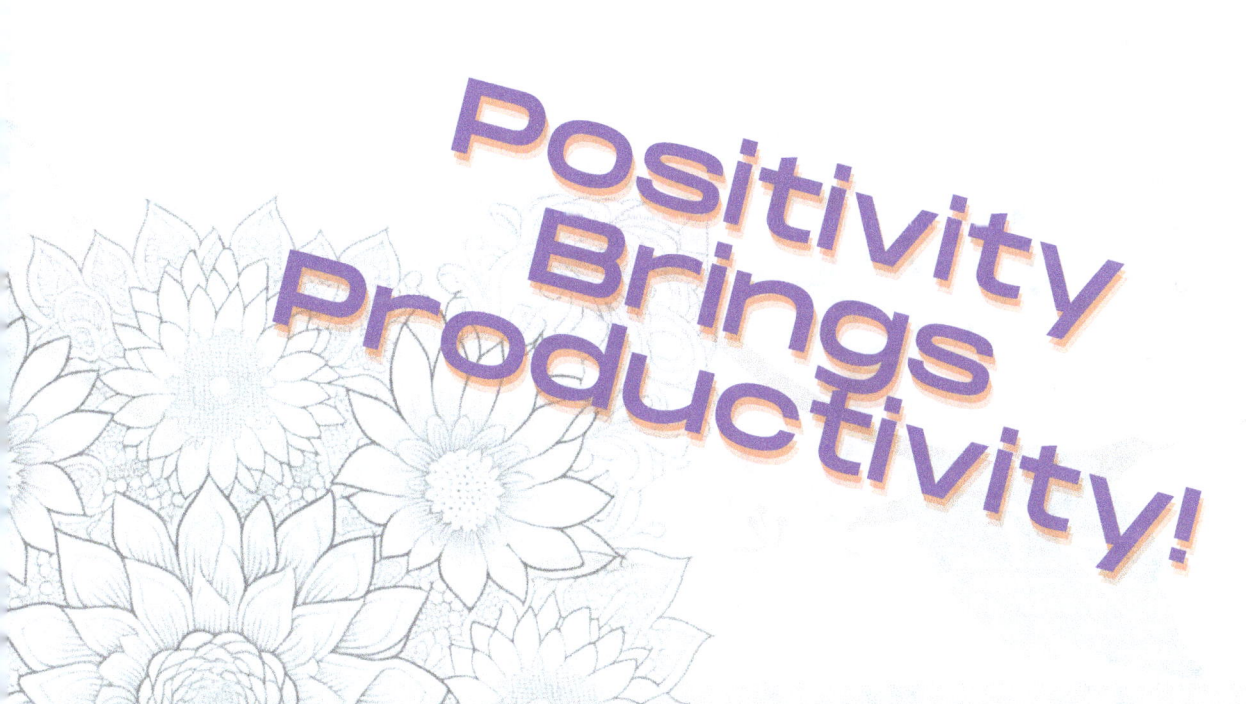

Positivity Brings Productivity!

The city of positivity!

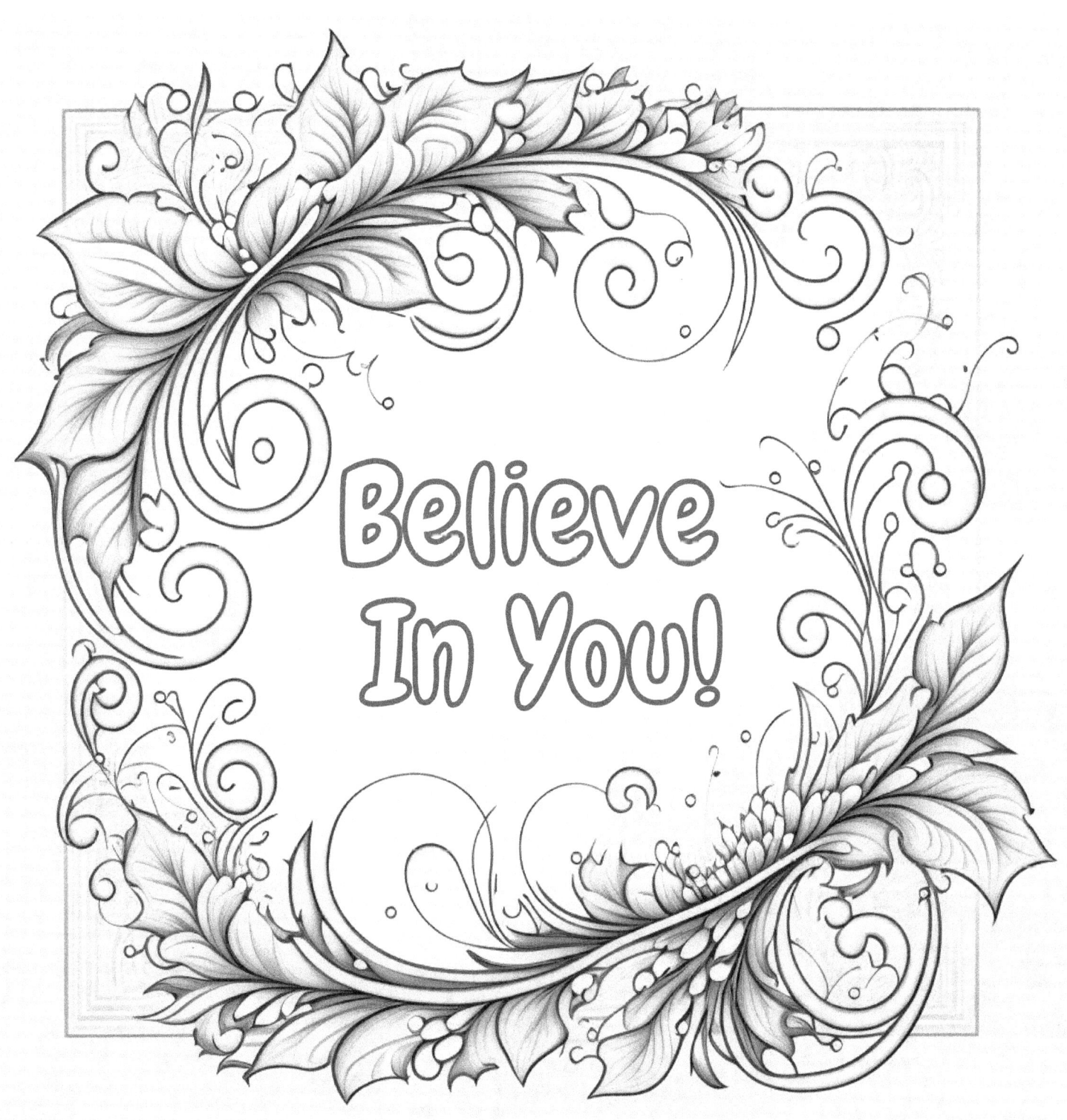

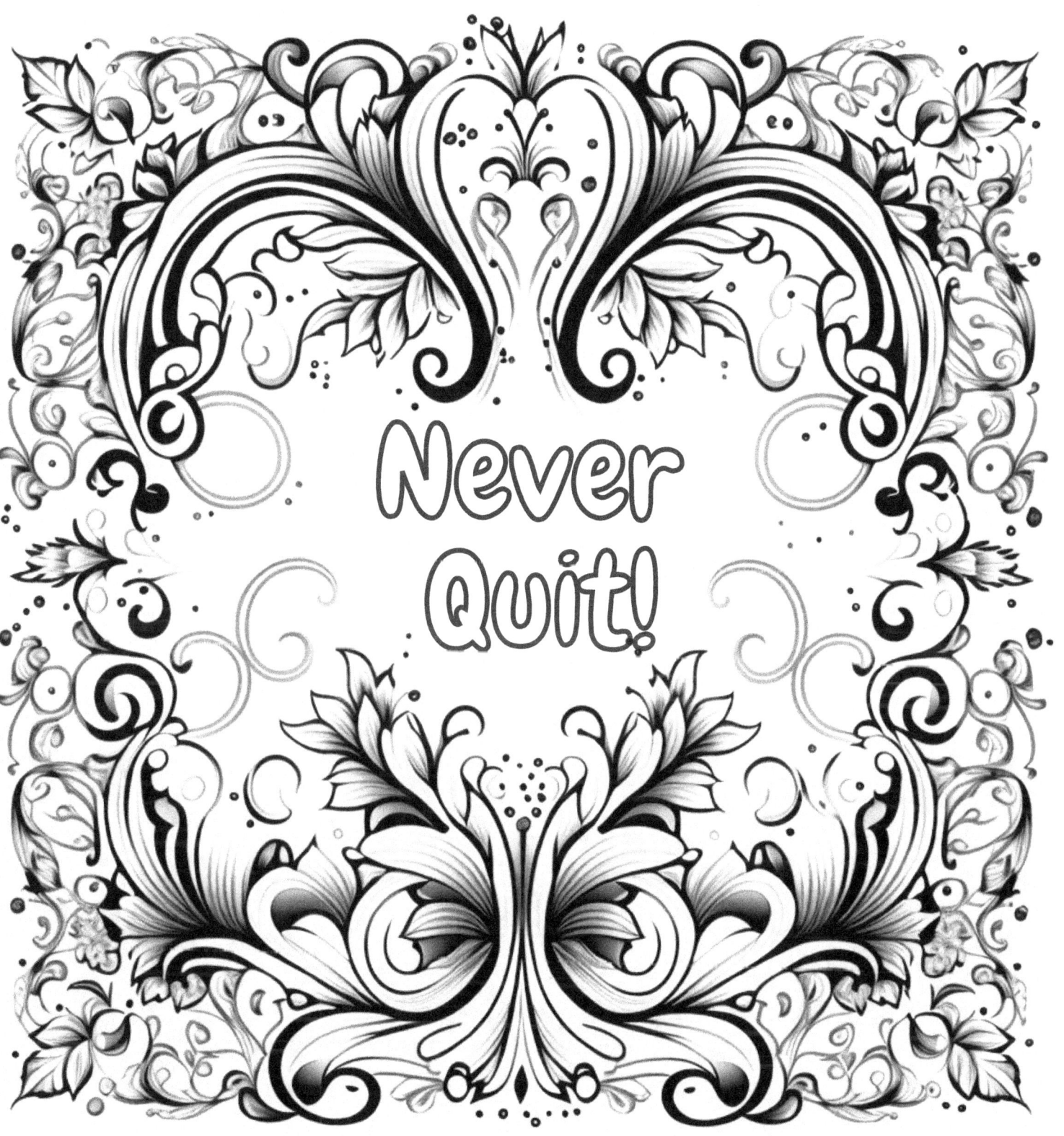

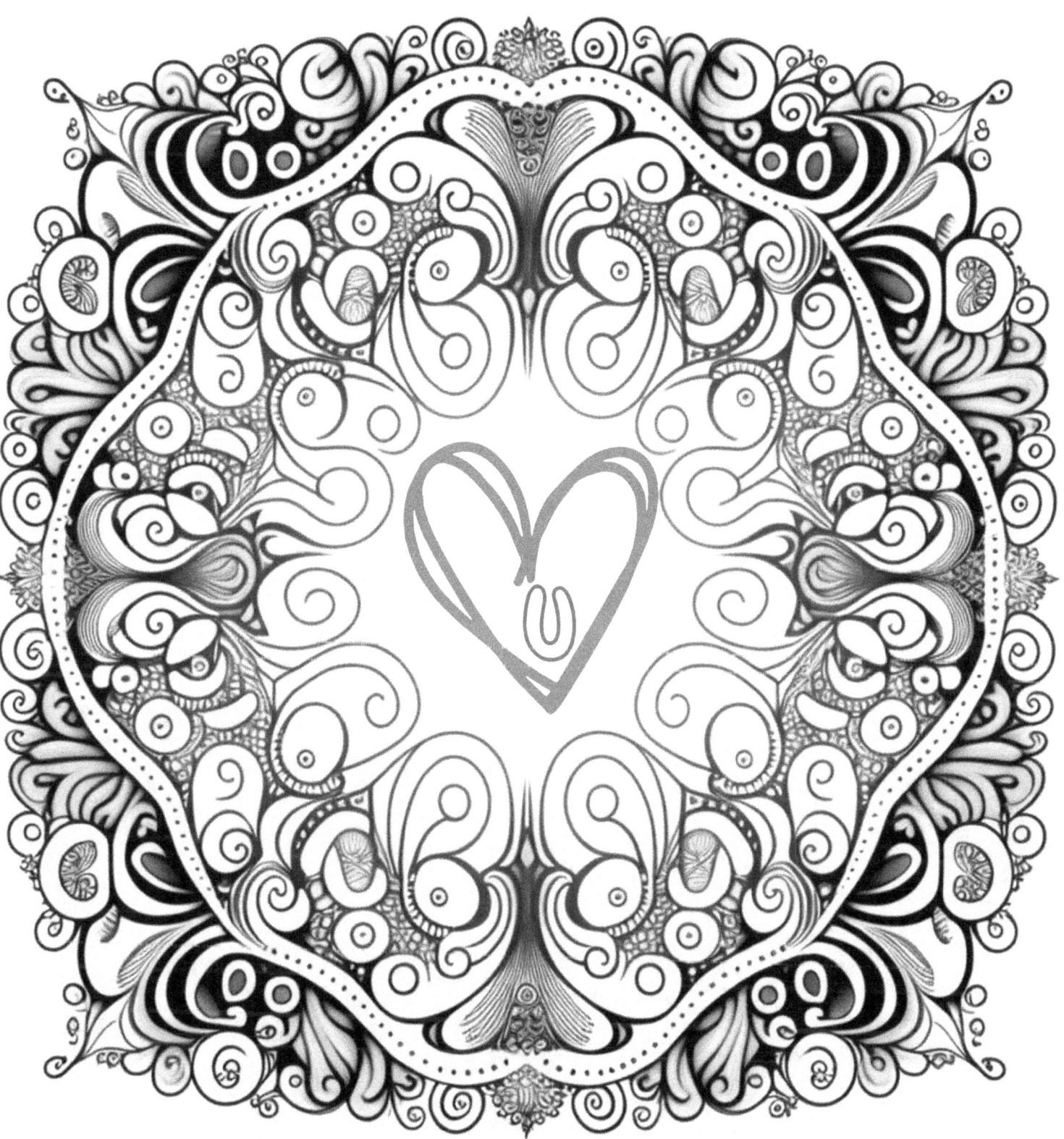

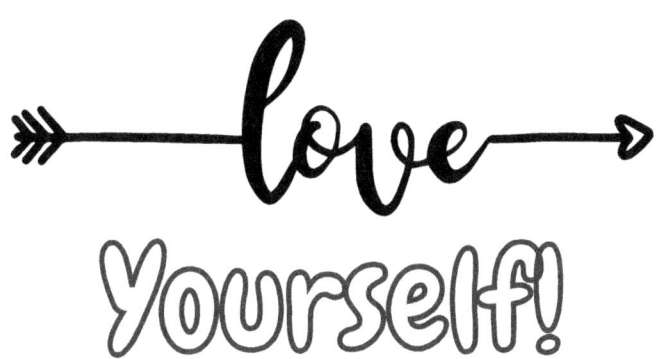

Yourself!

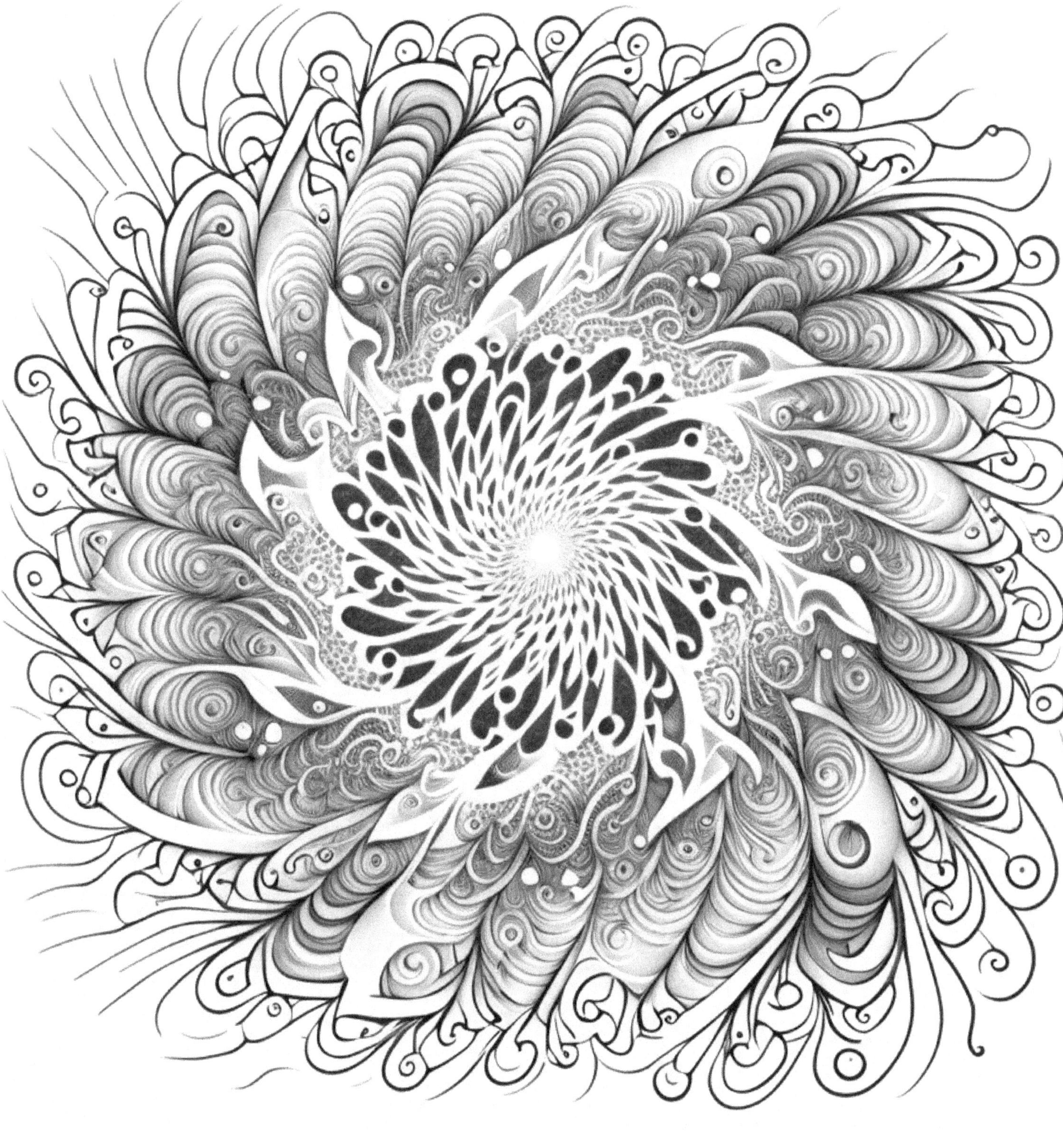

Adventurers Update!

We have arrived safely at the CITY of "Adventures!"

It is time to take bolder steps into unfamiliar territories!

Be bold, and courageous, you are an Expert!

.

Take Off!

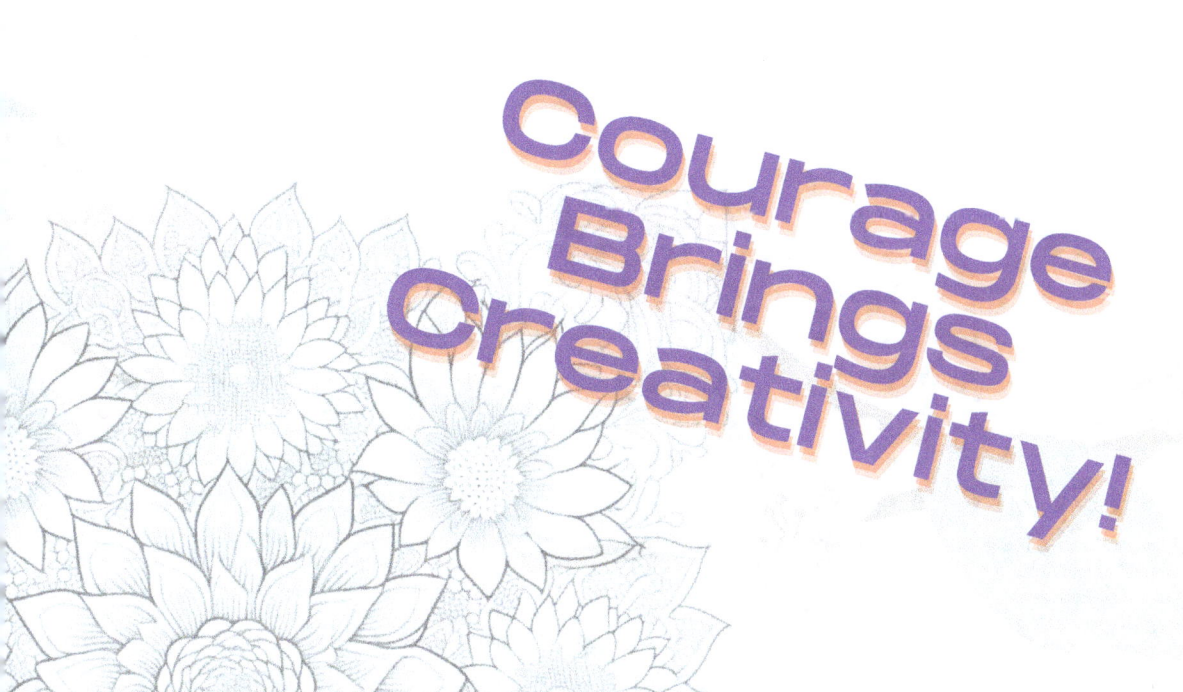

You are multidimensional!

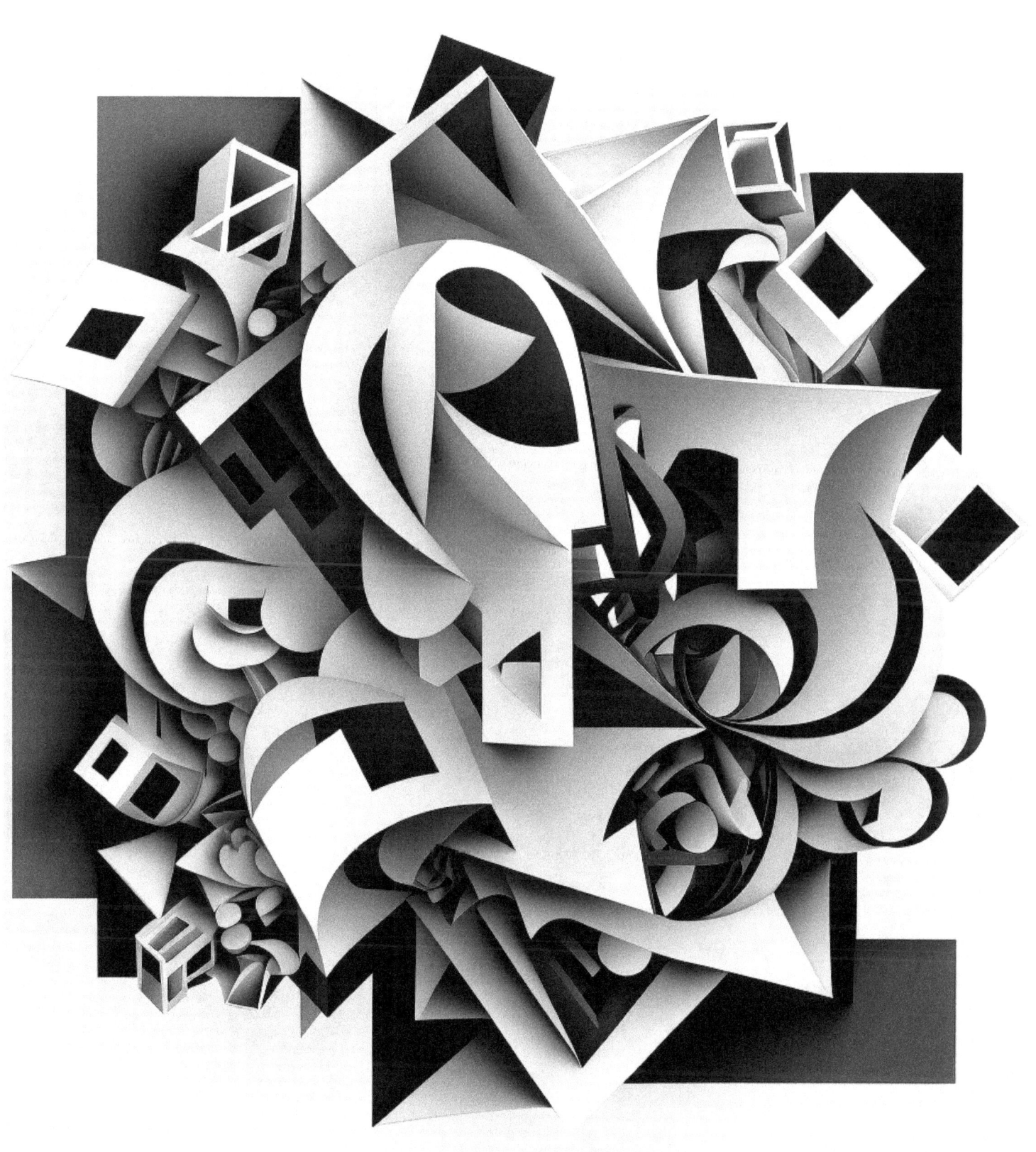

Crank up
Your Imagination now!

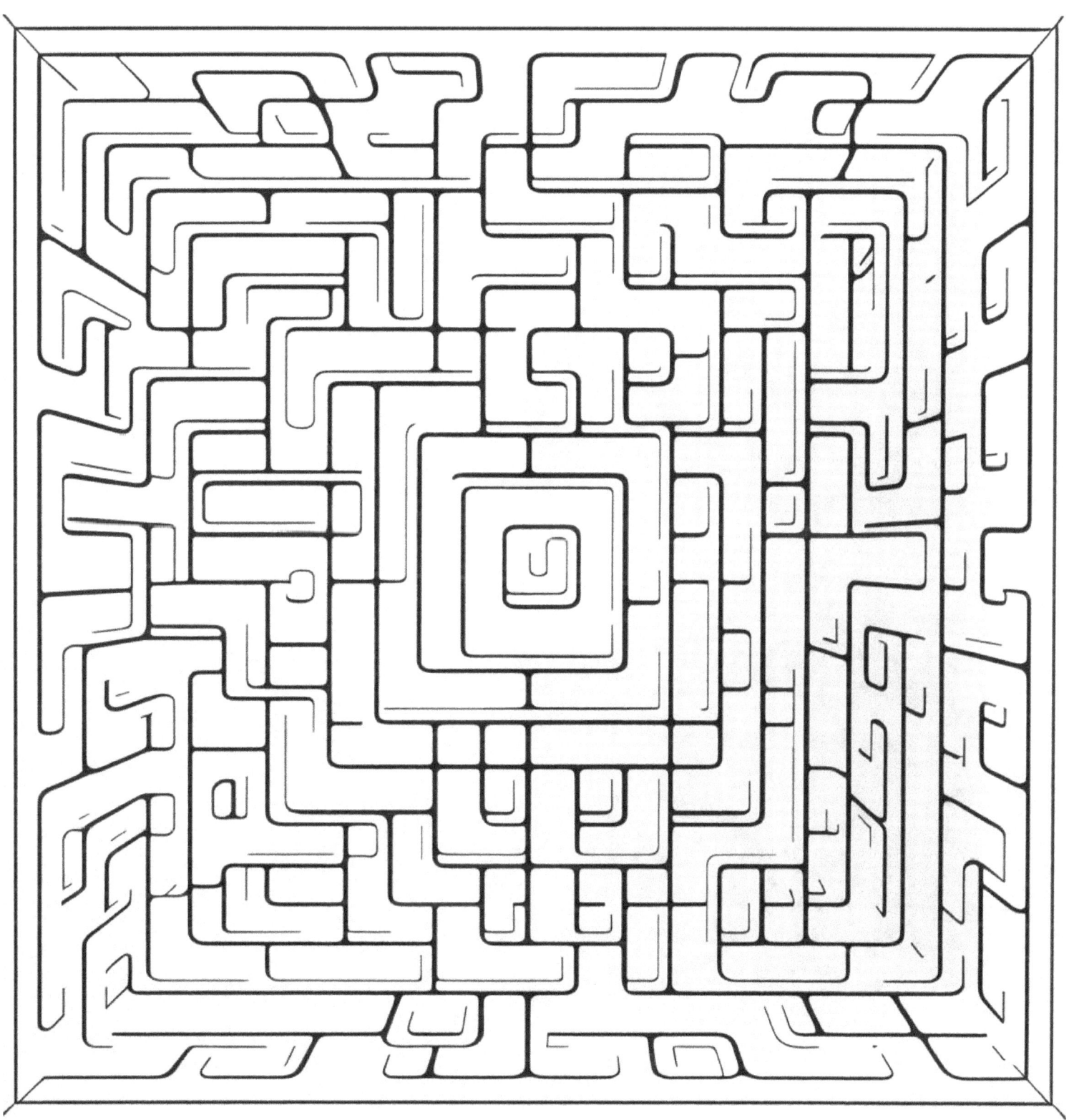

Go further, deeper!

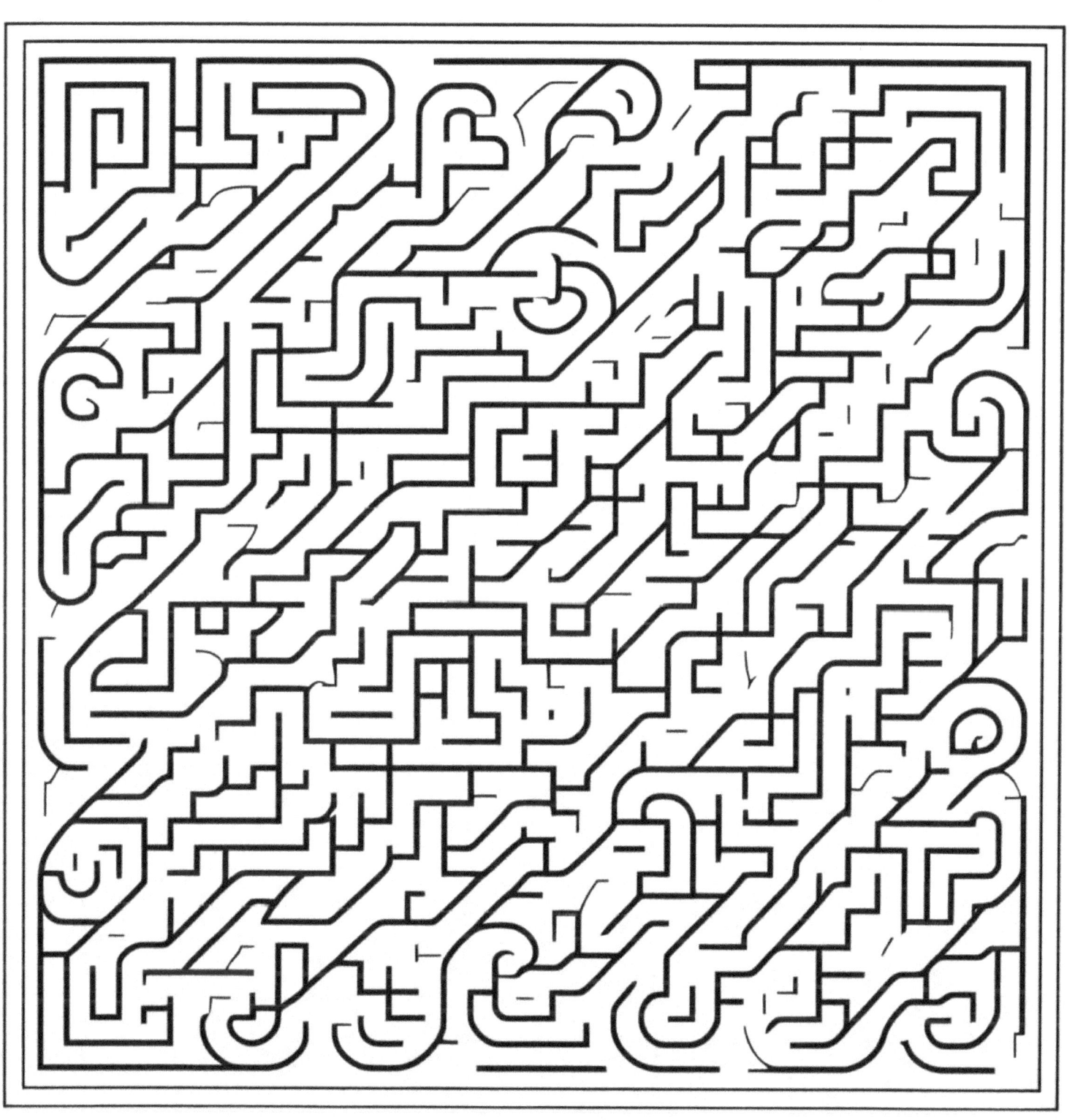

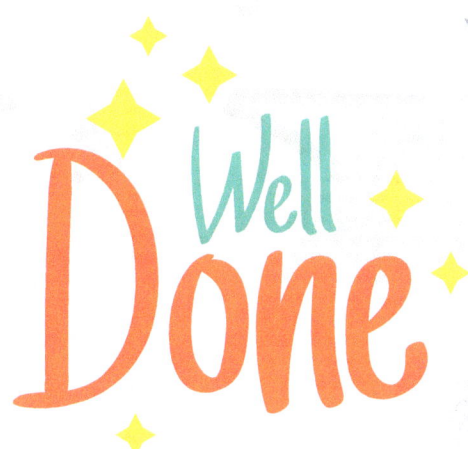

We and the Expert have arrived!

We are proud of You!

---•◆•---

Hey, do not be a stranger.
Let us keep in touch, after all, we just completed an adventure together.

Visit us at:
www.InspireLife.nft

You have to use Brave Browser or Opera Browser to open the website above.

It was great journeying with you!

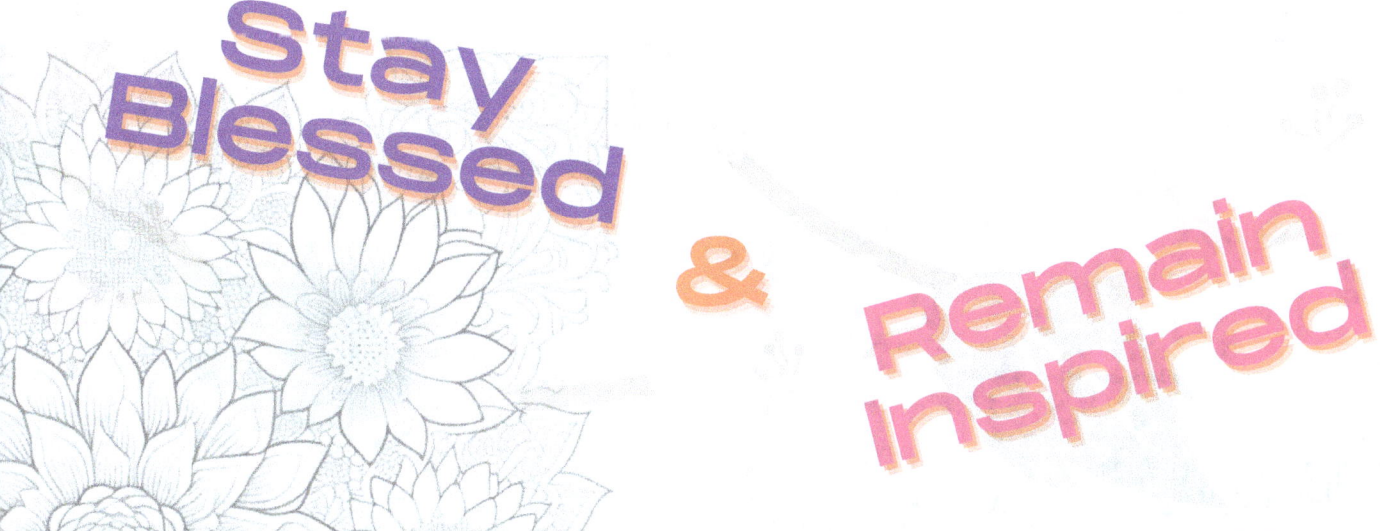